EARS OPEN, MOUTH SHUT:

15 Lessons You Don't Have to Learn the Hard Way as a New Entrepreneur, So Listen Up

A Warriors Guide Book
By Mike Ognek

Table of Contents

Table of Contents

Introduction

Like most entrepreneurs, I have a little Jekyll and Hyde in me. That analogy can apply to a lot of different aspects of an entrepreneur's life. We tend to travel a squiggly path between brilliance and madness from time to time and manage to hit all the points in between. If you are, or have ever been, in a relationship with an entrepreneur, you have certainly witnessed this first hand and most likely see it more clearly than the entrepreneur can.

For me, if you add in the fact that my wife and I have three young children, the time I spend towards the Hyde side of the spectrum is probably greater than the Jekyll side. On top of that, the time I spent in the Marine Corps created a stage of Hyde that, when reached, causes him to don a uniform and shout various metaphors about life, leadership, and simply getting things done. My wife, kids, and business partners love that guy.

The point is that the life of most every entrepreneur is not one of stability and constants. Cash flows change, markets change, ideas die and are born faster than the speed of our brains, just to name a few. In my first book, "Maneuver Management: Planning and Communication for Business Success," I laid out a concept called the "Pendulum" which describes how business's must manage their cycles in order to avoid states of crisis. Basically, identifying an operating zone and shifting that zone, when appropriate, achieves this.

Entrepreneurs have to manage their lives in a similar manner. Many things in life can create crisis without our assisting in their creation. Bad things happen to good people, there's not much we can do to prevent that. We can prevent crisis that are created by our own action or inaction though. That's what this book is about, so let's get started.

Chapter 1

Ears open, mouth shut.

I will start with a sort of odd admission. I never read book introductions. When I sit down to read a book, I want to get right into the material and find, more often than not, that the introduction is a story about the writer writing the book, their motivation, their background, etc. Quite frankly, I'm just not interested in that. If I read a really good book, I may go back and read the introduction afterwards, but that's a rarity too.

I have found that if an author writes that same material in the first chapter, I read it. Why? Because it's the first chapter, that's why. Did you read my introduction for this book? It's okay if you didn't; I wouldn't have either and it's my book. If you did, consider this your "re-introduction." Believe it or not, there's a point to my rambling, but you'll have to wait for a few chapters on that and just accept this as a book reader's confession, my penance being that I actually wrote an introduction, regardless of how short it was.

On to the meat. If you read "Maneuver Management," you know my background already. If not, shame on you and go buy it. In the meantime, "My name is Mike and I'm an entrepreneur." Not to blow smoke up or out of my own pipes, but after some face plants I have become pretty good at what I do. That's true for my own businesses as well as for the businesses I work with everyday. I'm also a former Marine Officer and one of the greatest factors of my success has been, and continues to be, the tools I received and honed while serving as a Marine.

Those early face plants I mentioned occurred for two reasons: I had some lessons to learn about running a business, e.g. being an entrepreneur, and I failed to realize the lessons I learned as a military officer were directly applicable to running a successful civilian business. Once I gained the knowledge and realized that, respectively, I got to a point where I could stop wearing a facemask to prevent permanent damage. Stumbles and knee scrapes still occur on occasion, but that's just part of the process.

Where Maneuver Management covered the latter, the earlier of those two reasons is what this book is about: gaining knowledge. You see, the cold hard truth is that you are not the first person to do what you are doing. Sure, your product could be the most innovative and original invention ever seen by mankind, but in order to make it a reality, you need to be an entrepreneur. Entrepreneurs, my friend, have been around as long as commerce; you are not the first.

That's an important point, so let it sink in. No, really. Stop reading and let that sink in. Okay, sunk? If you, during your sinking in period, realized that's important because you don't have to try to figure everything out from scratch then you are already ahead of the game- if you follow up on that. If you didn't get that, pay very close attention.

No matter what your product, service, or idea is, you have to launch your business in order to get it to market. If you are thinking, "But I just want to sell or license my idea to a big company and make millions," you are probably not an entrepreneur. Maybe you're an inventor, but not an entrepreneur. There's absolutely nothing wrong with being an inventor, but entrepreneurs have a seemingly inherent desire to suffer through the development, growth, and success of their companies. Many of us find more joy in the business than in the actual product or service. Many salespeople are like that too; they just love selling, no matter what they are selling.

For a new entrepreneur, the actions you take or fail to take during the startup of a new business can dictate success or failure. Wrong decisions early on can hinder you for years, even if you are successful. If you are not successful, they just may bankrupt you.

After years of starting, operating, and expanding businesses as well as helping others do the same, I have learned some hard lessons. Those lessons didn't have to be hard learned though. Recall my statement about applying the lessons I learned in the military. That was one of them.

Every Marine goes through basic training: Boot Camp for enlisted Marines and Officers Candidate School for officers. Every one of us could write a novel using all of the, sometimes unintelligible, spewing's of our Drill Instructors or Sergeant Instructors. Many are funny and many are not.

Some, however, are truly wise. Every so often a new phrase or gilded insult gets added to the Instructors repertoire of one liners, but a brand new Marine can sit down with an "Old Corps Marine" and chances are they heard the same things- although the older Marines probably got a lot more curses thrown at them and even a few fists. Even with changes to the vernacular, the lessons remain the same.

One of the phrases I learned from a finer instructor of mine at OCS was, "God gave you two ears and one mouth for a reason- listen more than you talk." After a few days it turned into a command, "EARS OPEN, MOUTH SHUT."

Whether he realized it or not, what he was really saying is that he knew more than we did, so we should listen. We didn't have a choice, so we listened, but the lessons he was conveying certainly served us all well. We didn't know what we didn't know, but we had over 200 years of history and experience behind us that was going to tell us what we needed to know and then exactly how to do it. Certainly, neither the idea or quote were his originally, but that was the first I had ever heard it.

Imagine if military officers were allowed to act like most entrepreneurs, trying to figure everything out from scratch. Our military would be in shambles. Instead of being the most powerful fighting force the world has ever seen, we would have an organization without organization, full of people wandering about trying to make things work. The occasional superstar would pop up and create successful pockets within the organization, typically from stumbling on the right answers or from hanging around long enough to figure things out.

Sound familiar? It should, that's what most entrepreneurs do- wander around trying to figure things out instead of tapping into the centuries of history and experience that is readily available from those who have traveled the entrepreneurial path before. Their companies lack organization, focus, goals, and proper decision-making because they're not taught the ways to find success and avoid failure. Part of that is not their fault, there's no mechanism in our society for teaching those things in a systemic manner. Part of that, is our own fault though. There may not be too many formal entrepreneurial programs out there and the ones that do exist probably won't teach you the basics, but there is plenty of knowledge and experience. We just have to seek it out and utilize it.

I'm not about to teach you about how to do your accounting or taxes and I'm not going to show you how to interpret your company financials. Basically, if you can learn it in a college or MBA class, it won't be in here.

Honestly, if you can learn it there, you can also learn it by typing a few words into the almighty Google.

What I am going to teach you is 15 things too many entrepreneurs do wrong. These are mistakes many of us have made. In fact, these are all lessons I learned very early on by doing the wrong thing. I have my MBA, so I can tell you first hand that you won't learn these in a classroom. I wish I did, but you won't. These are very basic things, some of which you may have already heard elsewhere, but I'm about to make them very clear. Now is the time to listen, before you make the same mistakes and lose time, money, and sanity or outright fail for lack of realizing others have gone before you and are willing to tell you what they did wrong so you can do it right.

Throughout this book, I refer to "new entrepreneurs" and "startup entrepreneurs." In many cases, they are one in the same. A new entrepreneur has to be a startup entrepreneur, necessarily. A startup entrepreneur, however, may be one that has already made a run at owning their own business and is doing it again. It may be that they failed the first time or just want to do it better on this go around. In a deeper sense, a new entrepreneur is also a startup entrepreneur in the sense that in order to get their business going, they must first get themselves started as an entrepreneur. So, in a way, they are launching a "self startup" and beginning their life as an entrepreneur. It is during this phase of their business life that they have the opportunity to build a foundation from which they can grow into a successful business person.

If you read Maneuver Management or any of the articles on our website (www.thewarriorsgroup.com), then you may be saying that my tone is a bit different in this book. You'd be right. This is startup basic training and Mr. Hyde has his uniform on. Ironically, if you read the introduction you would know what that means and why it's ironic. Tough love is still love; it just hurts a little more.

So, "**EARS OPEN, MOUTH SHUT!** Listen up, this may just save your (entrepreneurial) life!"

Chapter 2

Lesson I

Where's the remote?

How many times in your life have you asked "Where's the Remote?' How about, how many times have you asked repeatedly where it was while you spent 15 minutes looking for it and walking by the TV half a dozen times only to find out it was right under your nose, or cushion? Several I'm sure.

There are three types of people who lose remotes:

Type I- The first will do the above and search until they find it, wasting minutes or even hours.

Type II- The second will just get up and change the volume or channel to bypass their need for the remote.

Type III- The third will find a solution so they never have to look for the remote again. For me, that was installing a Bluetooth converter and an iPhone app so I could control my system no matter where my little crumb snatchers cached the remote this time.

In my less than qualified psychoanalytical application of naming conventions, I call Type I's the Hidebound, Type II's the Regressive, and Type III's the Entrepreneurs.

Just like the excitement a Hidebound feels when they finally find the remote, excitement about your new business is a really good thing. Deciding to make that leap into your own business is like an endorphin rush mixed with a shot of adrenaline and chased with a metal pail of shucked raw nerves. It's exciting, no doubt about it. It can also be nerve-racking and stressful, for good reason.

You are about to put your financial, emotional, and perhaps even familial security on the chopping block and the only person who can stop the ax from falling is you. It's a lot of responsibility, but the thing to always remember is that you are in control. I don't mean that in a purple, fuzzy, feel-good, metaphysical sense. I mean what I said: you are in control. You decide what happens and what doesn't. You chart your course and make way. I could go on all day with clichés, and I probably will, but the point is, you really are in control even when it feels like you're not. Just keep one hand on the proverbial wheel and the other on the fast food you'll be eating a lot of for the next few months.

It's important to fully grasp this concept. Not everything is going to go your way and when it doesn't, you have to make the conscious decision to be a Hidebound, Regressive, or Entrepreneur. It's up to you to adjust and make it happen and you can either keep searching until you find what you lost in the first place, go back to your old ways, or find a solution that solves your problem more permanently. No one else is going to do it for you; you are in control.

There is a flip side to that too though. I'll say it again- YOU are in control. That doesn't just mean that you are in control of the good, the bad, and the ugly parts of your business. It's actually a statement of one of the aspects of being an entrepreneur that is so appealing to people. When you have your own business, you have more control over your entire life. You decide what you do and when you do it. You decide when you want to go to lunch or visit your kids at school. You decide when you work late (and you will) or go home early (and you will, eventually), because, you guessed it- you're in control.

As you get going in business, don't lose sight of what's important to you- your priorities. You may say that one of your drivers is your family, but if they never see you, you're not supporting your priorities. It can be really easy to justify compromising your priorities on the basis of the same priorities. It's a death spiral once you get into it and it takes a serious smack in the face to realize it and pull out of it before hitting the deck in a fireball. Sticking with the family example, it's really easy to say that you are working seven days a week, 20 hours a day to support your family because they are what's most important to you. If you ask them, though, I bet they would say they would rather have you in their life than supporting it from the outside.

That very example is what happened to me. My daughter was born a few months after I started my first business after the Marine Corps. I worked like a dog, all day, every day to make ends meet and "build a solid foundation" so I would be able to spend more time with my new baby girl. I came home early one evening for a special occasion. By "early" I mean that I came home late for dinner. The special occasion was her first birthday.

Bad daddy, I know. At the time though, I was able to justify all the hours and work. It was hard to swallow, but I could rationalize being gone before she woke up and coming home long after she and my wife were asleep. I was in the death spiral. Luckily, I got my smack in the face that night. It wasn't anything anyone said or did, it just hit me. The next day I was home for breakfast and then went to work, locked the doors, and got to work on fixing my business and my life.

Over the next few days, I figured a lot of things out, including the foundation of Maneuver Management. Most importantly for this lesson though, is that I figured out I was doing things "ass backwards." Once you start your business, you'll quickly learn that your personal life and business life become one. That's okay, so long as you don't fight it and approach it with the right perspective.

Like I said before and I'll say it again, and again, you are in control. If you are struggling with maintaining your priorities and running your business, you're fighting it and not controlling it. Certainly, you'll have scheduling conflicts and not get to do absolutely everything you want to do, at least early on. You may miss this or that, but that's no different than if you had a job still. In fact, you'd miss more if you did. The key is to keep your priorities your priorities, even at a granular level. If the decision is between meeting with a client to sign a big deal or making it home for your spouses famous chicken kabobs, go sign the deal and then buy him or her those fancy metal skewers so they don't have to use sticks from the backyard anymore, but make sure that if being home for dinner with your family is a priority then you're there 9 times out of 10. If the decision is between your weekly staff meeting and being at your kids first day of school, you run the business- reschedule the meeting and be with your kid.

Those examples probably sound pretty clear-cut right now. Wait though, in the heat of your entrepreneurial oven, illusions are common and things can get really blurry, really quick. It helps if you have a sponsor. Yes, a sponsor, just like a 12 step program. If you know a successful entrepreneur that's willing to be your sponsor, that's all the better. If you don't though, all you really need is a friend or family member who can shoot you straight and tell you when you're all "jacked up." Trust me, if things get bad, you won't see it until you come really close to hitting rock bottom. Your sponsor is there to tell you when you're off your personal track. Pick someone with thick skin, you'll get mad at them when they tell you things you don't want to hear and say things like, "You don't know what it's like," "What else am I going to do," "It's all on me," or the ever so popular, "Dude, I've got this."

If it sounds like an intervention, it pretty much is. Which is why it helps to have a conversation with your sponsor along the lines of, "No matter what I say, don't give me any." Let them know you're going to be pissed and reject everything they say, but to stick on you. There are no safe words here; they need to stick on you until you feel that smack in the face.

As for the "ass backwards" part, that's where perspective comes in. I figured out that although my business life and personal life had Vulcan mind melded together, there were two ways to structure that and I had chosen the wrong one. The wrong way is to integrate your personal life into your business. That is, having a personal life (family, friends, hobbies, exercise, etc.) within the minuscule cracks of time that exist in your business life.

The right way to do it is to make your business a part of your personal life. That is, build your business around your personal priorities and not the other way around. At the core, what that means is that if your business is crushing your personal life and priorities, you don't necessarily have to work more now to be able to free up more time later. That is seldom what ends up happening. Instead, you work more now and then work some more later. The correct action is to work differently within the time you have for your business.

I understand that you are saying, "It doesn't work that way." For most people, it doesn't, you're right. It's not because that is by design, however. It is because they don't know any better and when they figure it out it might be too late. By no means am I saying you should be on vacation everyday and only work a few hours. I am saying there are things you need to do and attend to in your personal life that should not be dismissed because you now own a business. If your business is your life, then pretty soon you won't have a personal life.

Working differently may mean employing different systems, getting better at time management, staying focused, hiring, controlling costs better, or any number of other things. We'll get into some of those things in later chapters; as you'll see many of these lessons tie together.

The funny thing about perspective is that it is usually gained by looking in the rear view mirror. It may help you in the future, but you really have to learn perspective. The bad news is there are a lot of excuses that you can find to overrule good perspective, whether it's internally or externally applied. The good news is you don't have to learn perspective from personal experience, you can learn it from others. Some more good news is that no one cares about what your excuses are, so you can trash them right now.

As for "Where the Remote is," I have no idea, have you looked under the couch? If you're an entrepreneur, you've already stopped looking and have a solution, even if its wire hangers tied together long enough to reach the TV.

EARS OPEN, MOUTH SHUT.

- You are in control.
- Maintain your priorities.
- Build your business around your life, not the other way around.
- Get a sponsor.
- Keep Perspective.
- Stop looking for the remote.

Chapter 3

Lesson II

The Trojan Horse.

I said in the last chapter that your excitement about your new business is a good thing; it still is. There is a catch though, and it's one that can save your business and your finances. I call it the Trojan Horse Strategy and the contradictory behavior is Kicking Down the Door.

There's a lot to be said for the concept conveyed in the tale of those sneaky, tasty-yogurt-making Greeks making their way into the city of Troy inside the infamous Trojan Horse. Faced with an insurmountable obstacle, they devised a solution for breaching the city and ending the conflict. Brilliant, if you ask me and even if you don't.

Their alternatives were relatively few. They could try to starve the enemy soldiers out, but the tale tells us that after 10 years of siege, the Greeks didn't have the supplies to do that and would have starved first. They could have sent onslaught after onslaught to try to scale the walls, but that had already proved ineffective and they were running low on resources. Finally, they could have just focused all their might and forces on breaking through the front door. The likely outcome of which would not have been in their favor. Oh, and they could have just given up and left, I suppose.

Startup owners face the same set of choices, kind of. The Trojan War isn't hanging in the balance, but we fight our own little versions of war to succeed. Chances are really good that you are not the only player in the market you are entering. If you are, and your product is a homerun, you'll have plenty of competition soon enough and many of them will be much better funded than you. But, as chances being what they are, you are likely entering a battle that is already being waged by other people and you're the new guy on the field.

So, what do you do? Do you try to scale the walls, burn the place down maybe? Do you send wave after wave in full out attrition? No, you don't. You sneak your way in.

First, here's the mistake. Entrepreneurs are fired up about launching their business. They have their business plan in hand and are ready to take on the world. They gear up, make themselves look big (more on that later), paint their faces, start speaking with a Scottish accent and run up to the door of the marketplace. They let out a giant war cry and extend a Herculean kick 4 inches below the doorknob. The door busts open and they run in screaming, prepared to beat the competition to death with their new widgets and make the population love them by nature or force. The only problem is, the room turns out to be empty. Someone forgot to tell everyone they were coming. The next day, the consumers still don't know or care about their product and the competitors have drawn a target on them.

On top of all of the unsustainable expenses and overhead they created by gearing up and trying to look big, they now also get a nice bill for the door they kicked in and a ticket for disturbing the peace. No cheering in the street, no ticker tape parade. Just a shredded up door, a lot of bills, and a bunch of paint they can't get off their face.

It's in our makeup as entrepreneurs to want to create the ultimate solution. That includes solutions for every aspect of managing and operating our businesses. We tend to think about all of the things we may need and then seek to acquire them rapidly to be positioned for all possible conditions. This is especially true of new entrepreneurs and one or few person shops.

We're confident in our product, or else we wouldn't be launching a startup. We tend to see the positive outcomes and plan for them more than we plan for the negative outcomes, again especially true of new entrepreneurs. There's a lot to be said for that, in a positive way. Being able to envision a positive end state assists us with developing a pathway to get there. It also helps us stay positive when the going gets tough.

The downside is that trying to enter a market by kicking down the door is rarely necessary and even more rarely prudent. Although the level at which you launch is largely determined by the funding you have, even if you have a deep wallet, going too big, too fast, can still kill your business.

The key to this is market share. Market share costs. It can cost money, it can cost time, and it can cost both simultaneously. It doesn't just cost to get market share, but it costs to keep it too. Therefore, the more market share you have, the more it costs to keep it and even more to grow it.

Even if you did kick down that front door and found yourself surrounded by foes blocking your way to the masses of consumers, beat them back and gained a nice chunk of market share, you are now fighting a battle that you are ill prepared to sustain. You don't know how the consumers will react to your product longer term. You don't know what competitors have in their pipeline that may render your product old news. You don't know what you don't know, not yet anyway.

In comes the Trojan Horse. The Greeks slipped just a few soldiers into the city. If their effort failed, they would not have lost a great amount of resources. They could have reassessed and tried another solution. If it succeeded, however, they would have gained entry into the city without a fight, which is what the tale tells us happened, of course.

They pulled back their forces to fain retreat, with one soldier being "left behind" to offer the Horse. They looked small and non-threatening. The city of Troy opened up for the Horse and the rest we all know. The point is that they gained a small market share, without risking a lot of resources. Once they had that market share and saw the returns (adding in a little poetic license to relate to business), they funneled more resources into the city and took it from the inside out. As their soldiers gained more and more share of the city, they filled the void behind them with more and more soldiers, until they controlled the whole thing.

If you'll grant me a little greater license, the time the soldiers spent inside the city, concealed in the horse, was invaluable. During that time, they had the opportunity to gain awareness, e.g. knowledge. They were able to observe the city, the soldiers, and the citizens. They saw how they behaved, where they were, how they were armed, and how they reacted and interacted with each other. If they were able to pass that back to the main forces, wouldn't it have been invaluable information?

The same is true for you. By being small when you enter a market, you can gain a small fraction of market share, with little risk to your resources. You may not succeed the first time, but you'll have plenty of dry powder left to make another go using a different strategy or methodology. You won't paint a giant target on your back for your competitors. If you are entering a market with long time, well established players, they're probably tired of beating each other up all the time and look forward to new people popping up for them to pummel. They didn't become well established by being passive, so count on them being aggressive to perceived risks.

As I mentioned, we'll talk more about trying to appear big in a later chapter, but I do want to say this for now, appearing like you are a big, well staffed, advanced organization is much more important to you than it is to your consumers.

EARS OPEN, MOUTH SHUT

- Don't go kicking down any doors just yet.
- Market share costs to obtain and also to keep.
- Don't make yourself a target before you're ready to be one.
- Sneak in, take some notes, and then send in the forces.
- Appearing big is more important to you than it is to your consumers.

Chapter 4

Lesson III

Overnight success takes a long time.

We'd all be lying if we said we haven't daydreamed about thinking up a product that hit the market the next day and was an instant, runaway hit that made us a million dollars in the first 24 hours. Well, wake up and start working.

There is no such thing as an overnight success. I used a period at the end of that statement, in case you hadn't noticed. As in, "There's no such thing as an overnight success- period." Movies hit the theatres and make millions on opening night, but it took months or years to make them. Singers get picked up at a local gig and record a smash single, but they had been playing that same $50 gig for 5 years. Books sell tens of thousands of copies the day they are released, but they take a long time to write, trust me on that one.

It goes on and on. What the public may call an overnight success is really just the moment the product becomes successful. There are untold hours and dollars in that products conceptualization, development, manufacture, distribution, and so on. Maybe winning the lottery qualifies, but it seems even those winners manage to screw that up and end up broke, in jail, or both. They probably played many times before winning too.

The bottom line is that success is a process; it is systematic action focused on achieving certain results. It's a process that, for some, accelerates rapidly and they find themselves beyond where they thought possible. For others, it's a process that takes years, or even a lifetime. For others still, it's a process that never completes.

The tough love here is that it doesn't matter what your product or service is, if you are a new entrepreneur, you are going to have to drip some sweat on the floor. Whether that sweat is actual sweat, just a steady flow of tears, or looks a lot like dollar bills, will depend on your product, experience, and resources. I single out new entrepreneurs here for a reason. As an entrepreneur grows, we learn how to sweat less. Part of what I am trying to teach you here is how to do that from the get go. No need to get dehydrated and pass out everyday, though it may be necessary on some. Entrepreneurs who have already successfully launched a business and are engaging in a new startup will typically have connections, experience, and resources not readily available to newbies, which also allows us to sweat a little less. Another one of my Sergeant Instructors used to say, "Work smarter, not harder." As you gain experience in your business, you'll learn how to work smarter, not harder.

If the fact it's going to take a while sounds like bad news, it really isn't unless you only have 2 months of capital and it's going to take you 12 months to start turning a profit. It's not bad news because you can go into your startup knowing, without a doubt, you're going to have to sweat; I just told you. I hope you only sweat profusely for a very short time and find great success, but recognize, acknowledge, and accept the fact that it's okay to need an IV drip once in a while to re-inflate your veins and get rid of that splitting headache because you sweat all you could sweat that day.

If you said, "No kidding Mike, I know I am going to have to work for it," then good for you. You are either truly prepared for this aspect of your endeavor or you have no idea what it actually means. For the latter, there's bliss in ignorance, so enjoy it while it lasts. If you question the fact that you are going to have to put in a lot of hard work to succeed, then you need to go look in the mirror and watch yourself deliver repeated blows to your soft tissue areas until it sinks in.

Whether you really understand that now or discover it in earnest in the coming days, weeks, and months (even years), remember not to digest and react to that epiphany in isolation. Stay in control and keep your priorities; work smarter, not harder.

In the first chapter, I told you that there are a lot of people who came before you and walked the same path you are about to. They can help you sweat less too. Here's some more tough love- your business is the same as everyone else's. No? Tell me about a business problem you are having and I'll show you that same problem in a dozen other businesses that are on the same street as you.

So, lets go through some of the objections you are having to that statement. We can skip the fundamentals like accounting, record keeping, staffing, advertising, not having enough time, and being broke. It should be abundantly clear that most entrepreneurs have those same issues. What if you're developing software and are having problems integrating your platform into other industry standards? You had better believe every other software developer has had that same problem. Are you developing a new piece of technology? Yes, other businesses have struggled with finding the right components, integrating and assembling them, and finally manufacturing it. Are you doing something entirely new, for you, and have to figure out a vast array of pieces to make it all work? Welcome to business.

The list is long and comprehensive. Crappy vendors, crappy clients, and crappy employees; market crashes, system crashes, and car crashes; piles of regulation, piles of bills, and piles of other piles. We all feel the same pain; it's how we deal with it that allows us to succeed. We can either create a new system or process to accomplish what we need to or we can look for answers from all of those who have already done this. We can seek out people that are successfully doing what we need to do and get the answers without sweating nearly as much.

Of course, your direct competitor is not going to help you find the answers, but you don't need them too. Remember, all businesses have the same problems. Look for people outside of your industry or niche who are successful at navigating the challenges of the specific issue you are facing.

Here's a great example from one of my own businesses. My partner and I, who is also my brother, decided we were going to develop, manufacture, and sell a particular type of equipment. We created a list of products we wanted to make, spent the time working out the designs, and then started to look for manufacturers to produce our products.

That's when "it" happened. If this is not your first startup, then you know what "it" is. "It's" that moment when you see all of the complexities and hurdles facing you and the wind dies out of your sails. "It" happens to even the most seasoned entrepreneurs every time we enter a different category of business. We had tons of product designs, the chutzpa to make it happen, and the business experience to do it successfully, but "it" still happened.

"It" is the killer of more startups than most anything else. In fact, "it" kills startups before they even start. Some people just can't put the puzzle pieces together or work through the fog; they don't pull the trigger and never go forward. For others, "it" is coupled with the realization that their overnight success is going to take a long time and they are really going to have to work at it.

My partner and I have experience in ecommerce, advertising, and operations, just to name a few. This wasn't our first rodeo. The "it" was about finding the components we needed, or where we could have them made to our specs, then getting all of the components to a different factory to be assembled, then getting all of those products onto a ship, sailed across the oceans, cleared through customs, put on a train, taken off the train, put on a truck, and delivered to our facility so we could sell them. We had never done that and were looking at a giant logistical puzzle with players ranging from factories, freight handlers, foreign governments, our own government customs regulations, and insurance companies, just to name a handful. There were warehouses overseas, on the west coast, and on the east coast that all had a part to play in getting our equipment from there to here.

Fortunately, since we had ridden a few horses before, we knew "it" was coming, we just didn't know what "it" looked like. A new startup is kind of like watching a bad horror flick. People are disappearing, the walls are splattered with blood that looks a lot like cheap ketchup, and there are signs of a beast as the culprit. We have no idea what that beast looks like yet, save maybe a glance at a foot or tail. We know that beast will make it's appearance at some point in the movie though, so we're prepared for it and looking out for it. Once we see it, we can take it all in and react accordingly.

Experienced entrepreneurs are like seasoned horror flick fans, they know the plot, but not necessarily what the characters will look like. New entrepreneurs are like a teenager getting to see their first horror movie. They have no idea what's coming and when it does, it surprises the hell out of them. They may like that experience and go back for more, or that may make them run out of the theater screaming and never watch another horror movie again.

So, there we were, sitting in a dead zone on the open ocean of our new project. As we were sailing out there, we could see tons of boats just drifting on the horizon. As we got closer, we could see all of the abandoned vessels in the dead zone. These were the people who ran into "it" and never made it through. Since we knew it was coming, though, we packed plenty of gas and after charting a course, we started the engine and motored the hell out of there.

The key is in how we charted that course. If you haven't figured it out, by the way, I like analogies and metaphors; it's the poetic side of me trying to come out, I guess.

We didn't build a plane and a launch deck to fly out and map out the ocean for masses of land. We picked up the radio and phoned a friend. It just so happens this friend owns and operates a successful import business. We didn't need someone who knew how to make our equipment, we just needed someone who knew how to make shit in general and then get it from there to here.

You may be saying, "But there are companies out there that do all of that for you." Yes, there are, but the simple fact is they charge too much and are a real pain in the ass to work with as an entrepreneur creating new products. Remember the Trojan Horse too, going in big and spending a lot of money with a company to do all of that for you is not in keeping with sneaking in and risking less. Besides, learning new things is part of the fun of starting new businesses.

Our friend quickly connected us with his system for sourcing materials and factories and gave us a down and dirty lesson on the logistics of putting those pieces together. He introduced us to his Customs Broker. His what? Exactly. If you're unfamiliar, these are people who make sure your stuff is where it's supposed to be, when it's supposed to be there, and gets kept out of import jail for lack of proper paperwork or duty payments. Finally, he gave us his freight handler information, the folks who actually move your stuff from there to here, in and out of warehouses, on and off of ships, trains, and trucks, and right to your font door.

We found someone who had done all of this before and opened up our ears. Because of that, we had a lot less sweating to do in figuring all of that out on our own. We would still sweat a bit, but not nearly as much as we would have otherwise. As a startup entrepreneur, you don't get the benefit of corporate knowledge retained within an organization. You can't go down the hall to "Bill's" office and ask who you need to call to get X, Y, or Z. The good news is that as a startup entrepreneur, you have access to the collective experience and knowledge of those who have already done it, and that is much more valuable than any "turnover binder" sitting in a dusty cubicle. We were lucky in this instance, because we already knew someone who had the knowledge. Even for us, though, that's a rarity. Just like you will have to do, we still have to seek out people who know what we need to know and are willing to share it. More good news: they are all over the place. If you're a social recluse and don't know anyone at all, turn to the internet. There are myriad groups and forums with people who have the experience and want to share it. Look specifically at professional networking sites, like LinkedIn, and start joining groups related to your endeavor or issue.

EARS OPEN, MOUTH SHUT

- Overnight success doesn't exist.
- You will sweat.
- Your problems are not unique.
- Seek out others who know what you need to know, don't reinvent it.
- Wear a raincoat and pack extra gas, "it" happens.

Chapter 5

Lesson IV

Catfish get really big, but they're still tasty.

Noodling. What the hell is that all about? I just don't get it. I'm not judging; if you want to stick your arm up an underwater hole in hopes an enormous fish will think you're dinner, have at it. I just don't get it. Noodling has absolutely nothing to do with what I'm about to tell you. I just needed to get that off my chest.

First, truth be told, I don't eat catfish. I don't like it Sam I am, no matter where it's from or where you want me to eat it. Not going to happen unless I'm in a desperate survival situation and even then I'm looking for anything else before eating one of them. All of my seafood related baggage doesn't change this lesson though.

If you've spent anytime surfing the web, you've probably seen pictures of catfish larger than the person holding them. Where I come from, Northern New Jersey (fist pump), catfish live in the ponds and streams and are the size of a newborn kitten. It seems like the further south you go, the bigger they get. Here in Northern Virginia, where I live now, they're more the size of lions. Even further south, they are similar in size to Jaguars- as in the car, not the cat. Here's the thing though: they taste the same.

How do I eat a giant catfish? I don't, but you can by taking it piece by piece. I do, however, approach the complexities of a startup with the same methodology. There's a lot to do when you're starting a new business, even more if it's your first one. There's forming the company, getting banking set up, navigating regulations, obtaining licensing, and a plethora of other things on top of actually bringing your product to market. You're probably like most startup entrepreneurs and are either a one-person show or pretty close to it. There's only one way to get everything done without getting overwhelmed- put a little on your plate and eat it piece by piece.

I'm pretty certain you've heard similar analogies to this, maybe, "How do you eat an elephant," or something like that. The difference in my catfish analogy is that you're going to listen this time, because if you don't, it's another thing that can kill your business before it even gets going. There are occasions where a business fails to correctly interpret the laws and regulations pertaining to their business and ends up getting shut down. That's rare though and when it does happen, the case, more often than not, is the business owner intentionally skirted the rules and that was not the only thing they were doing wrong.

All the details involved with a startup can kill your business for the same reason "it" can- you get overwhelmed and give up. There's no reason for that to happen. Let's look back at the EARS OPEN, MOUTH SHUT bullets from the previous chapters and pull a few out:

- You're still in control.
- Appearing big is more important to you than it is to your customers.
- Don't go kicking in any doors.
- Success takes sweat and time.

Remembering you are in control is important because starting up is a process and you need to control the process instead of letting it control you. Once you get past the idea of having to appear big, you can shave a few pages of tasks and "needs" off your to-do list and focus on what you really need to do to get up and running. You're not kicking in any doors, so you can also shave a few more pages off that list because you don't have to get all geared up. You'll also save a lot of money, which means you'll save a lot of stress, which means the startup process will be easier. You know you're going to have to sweat, but you also know you don't have to sweat for no reason at all. You also know success is going to take some time. That last one is important because time isn't just a pressure, with the right perspective it's an asset- your greatest asset. We'll get to more of that later. For now the point is that if it takes you a week to prepare for launch and then the next year fixing all your mistakes, you would have been much better off taking it piece by piece and spending a month to do it right. Not only is it good for your longevity, it's the right way to do things and avoid the frustration that leads to giving up.

Here's how you eat this giant, and I might add nasty, fish. You've probably already spent some time developing your concept. Before you do anything else, flesh it out. Stop worrying about business structure, websites, facilities, and everything else. Figure out exactly what your product is, and although I use the word "product," I am referring to whatever it is you believe people will pay you for- a service, a meal, whatever.

Once you have that, now find all of the state regulations that apply to the daily operation of your business. Remember, you don't have to start from scratch and we're talking about the daily operation of your business, not every aspect of your business. Talk to other business owners and seek out resources. Many states offer brief sheets on what you have to do to be in compliance. State Small Business Administration Liaisons are great resources too. You don't have to download and read the entire code of your state, work smarter. It might seem strange to do this at this point, but it's perfectly logical. Once you know what your product is, there may be specific regulations you need to comply with for your industry or product.

Let's say you want to open up a restaurant, for example. Your state probably requires you have a business license and a food service license. You'll have to have health inspections and perhaps make reports to the state or county you operate in. You'll probably have to collect and pay sales tax too. These all relate to the daily operation of your business. Stay focused, don't start following web links from site to site about all the complexities of running a restaurant, stick to the regulations for daily operation.

Make a list of everything you think you need to do and then spend some time digging into each of those requirements in order to ensure you actually are required to do them for your business. "Better safe than sorry" is a valid statement for some things, but "Better not sign up to be regulated unless you have to" is a better one. You're not looking to skirt the law here. You are looking to avoid unnecessarily raising your hand for things you don't have the time to deal with. The clearest example I can give you is that almost every new entrepreneur I meet thinks they need a business license for their state or county. In many cases, that's not true. It may not stay that way, but it may not be a requirement when you startup. In my state and county, any business earning less than $200k a year in gross receipts does not require a business license. On top of that, if you don't get a license and end up earning $200k or more that year, you can just get the license when that becomes clear to you and it's no harm, no foul. Not having to do that can mean a few less pages of paperwork, phone calls, trips to the county or state offices, or courthouse. It's one less thing to worry about and one less thing to pay for, which, by the way, you'll pay every year after you get it to keep it valid. Not only is it one less thing you have to do now, it's one less thing you have to do every year until you actually really need to do it.

With your list of actual requirements in hand, don't do anything. Not yet, for good reason of course. Now, learn the regulations that impact how your business gets what it sells. You may not have any regulations at all for this category. If you draw portraits of people, you're probably clear on this one. If you import and sell chemicals, you're going to be knee deep in it. Work smarter; seek out others who have done it before. Same deal here as with the state requirements- spend the time to dig deeper and figure out if they are really applicable to you.

Now that you know what you need to do, it's time to start your actual business entity. Why now? It will make your life easier, that's why. You'll need that to register your business, when and where required, get your banking set up, get your books going, and a lot of other little nitnoid items. Keep it simple. For most people, an LLC is more than adequate for conducting and protecting your business. If you have a more complex situation, you may need a specialized LLC like a PLLC or even an S or C Corporation. Now is the time to figure that out so you don't have to go back later and change the structure of your business; that's just more paperwork, time, and money.

Figuring this out is pretty simple, read about the different structures and benefits of each. Again, you'll likely find an LLC is appropriate, but you may find you need more than that. Where do you read about it? Online, of course. If you live in the boonies and don't have internet, there's a place called a library. Pretty cool places, these "libraries." They are full of books, have internet access, and no one is ever there.

After your research, if you still have a doubt, go with an LLC. Most states make it easy to convert from an LLC to a corporation, but not the other way around. If a need arises in the future, it will be a much less painful process. Also, unless you have extenuating circumstances, just form your company in the state you live and operate in. There are some legal benefits to registering in states like Delaware and Nevada, but the reality is you probably don't need that. Here's my disclaimer: I'm not a lawyer so seek competent legal counsel on this. Now that that's out of the way, just register in your own state. If you do go with an out of state formation, you'll still need to register with the state you operate in, so it's more paperwork, more time, and more money in the long-run. If a need arises and the situation warrants it, you can always move the company when you're making the big bucks. By that time, though, you'll probably realize it's not necessary. The exception to that may be if you live in California. It may be the most beautiful state in the Union, but if you live there, you know why I say that and why it might pay to form your business elsewhere. I love California, by the way, and it's a shame it's such a pain in the ass state for small business. I would be living there if it were friendlier in that regard.

There is an option for making this even simpler that may be appropriate: a sole proprietorship. If you don't plan on expanding much or making much money, go ahead and do that if you want. Otherwise, skip it. It is less work overall as far as administration goes, but there's no protection for you or your business and if you do grow past your expectations you'll have to do this all over again. I don't recommend it.

Once you pick your entity type, head over to the state website and fill out the forms for your choice. Send them in, or submit online if you can, and pay your fees. Then, sit back and wait. Yes, wait. Don't do anything else with setting up your business until you have the certificate of confirmation back from the state telling you that you are a registered business under the name you chose. If you go filling out other forms and registering for this and that and the state comes back telling you the name is already taken, you've wasted a lot of time, energy, and money on top of creating an unnecessary administrative burden to go and fix all of that. If you have some things left over from your regulatory research, which you shouldn't, go back and get clarification on those while you wait. Otherwise, just chill, you'll be busier than ever very shortly.

After you get your state certification letter, or email, get your EIN from the IRS. You should know what that is, but just in case, it's your Employer Identification Number. Basically, it's your businesses Social Security Number. It's simple, do it online at the IRS website, it takes 5 minutes and you will get your number right then and there. Print out the PDF they present you with, you'll need it. Some will tell you that you may not need to get an EIN, they would be wrong. As far as the law goes, you may not need one, but you are going to keep separate books for your business. You are going to file taxes like you are supposed to. You are going to have a business checking account and keep your company money separate from your personal accounts. You need an EIN to set up a bank account, so you need an EIN.

Got that? Good. Now, before you go and set up a bank account, how do you intend to get paid? Checks, PayPal, Credit Card on site? If credit cards are included in that list, you have some options. Will you need to collect payments online? If so, can you get away with using PayPal or Google Checkout or do you need a full fledged merchant account? Merchant accounts require a lengthy application and credit check as well as monthly account fees that can add up pretty quickly. Keep it simple; don't get one if you don't need one yet. If you decide you need one, you can set that up later.

If you don't need to take payments online or can get away with PayPal or Google Checkout, but still want to be able to take credit cards on site, take a look at services like Square. Services like Square offer free applications for your mobile phone, free card swipers, and no need for a merchant account. There are no monthly fees and the percent of the transaction they take is only slightly higher than a traditional merchant account. They are easy to set up and easy to use.

We looked at that first, because it's time to go to the bank and setup an account. Make sure you have your state certification letter and your EIN PDF printed out, or the letter the IRS will send you- it's the same thing. When you sit down at the bank, the representative will probably offer you all sorts of options for bank accounts and added services. You need a cheap checking account. You need online banking. Remote deposit is nice, but don't pay for it. You need a debit card. You don't need much more. Order your checks online from a vendor not associated with the bank and not at the bank or through their vendor, you'll save a lot of money. While you're there, if you decided you need a merchant account, talk to them about that. You already researched all of your options, so you're smart on what other companies offer as far as fees and services go. You'll be able to compare those rates and benefits against your bank and make a decision on the spot. If you decide to have it setup at the same bank, they will get you started right away and that will save you time and energy.

We're almost there. Put a nice chunk of money into that shiny new account and stop using your personal accounts for business expenses. You're in business now, you're not playing with an idea anymore and it's time to start acting like it. Every business expense from here on out should be paid for with your business accounts. If you need a credit card for your business, get one or use your checking debit card. If you run low on cash and need to use some more personal money, put it into your business accounts first and then use it. You'll be tempted to say that you'll remember what you did with the fancy accounting at the end of the year, but you won't. Keep it clean, keep it simple, work smarter.

Start keeping your books. Whether you do it with a program like QuickBooks or Peachtree is up to you, but I highly recommend it. It's easier for you and your accountant (more on that to come). Don't spend any more money until your books are up and running. Account for every dollar and cent into and out of your business using your books, no exceptions. If your books are wrong, your business is wrong, so do it right.

You may not know how to classify expenses and income correctly. That's okay, create an account for expenses called "Ask my Accountant," and do the same for income. Put everything you are clueless about in there and, well, ask your accountant. Don't wait until the end of the year to do it, but don't call them everyday either. Do it every month or quarter until you figure things out, which you will.

When you classify items in these categories, make good use of the notes and memo sections. Be sure to write an explanation of where the money came from or went, what it was for, and why you don't know where it goes in your books. You think you'll remember, but when you finally call your accountant and see that you have a hundred "Ask" items, you won't remember- trust me, I've been there.

How's that fish taste? Not too bad I'm guessing. Piece by piece and we've already eaten a whole fillet.

You're all set up with your business entity, banking, and books. Now, go ahead and start filing all of the other applications and paperwork you need to comply with regulations. I recommend taking a minute to put them in a logical order. You may need proof of registration from one to complete another, so it makes sense to figure that out now and press through them in an orderly and efficient manner. There will be some waiting time involved here. Take advantage of that by going back and gathering all of the expenses you incurred before you actually had your business set up. You'll want those at the end of the year for "Startup Expense" write offs. Your accountant can help you with the best way to treat those expenses, but you need to know what they are in order to treat them in any way at all.

Assuming you've got all of that out of the way, you're in compliance and ready to get going, it's time to map out the rest of your startup tasks. This is also something you can do while you wait on some of your regulatory filings.

For this part, what your list looks like will greatly depend on your business. The best case is that you have read, or will read, Maneuver Management and use the 5P tool for this portion of your startup planning. If you haven't and don't plan to, you can still use the resources section of our website (www.thewarriorsgroup.com) for some useful tools and examples of planning using the 5P. In keeping with everything I've said in this chapter, the 5P tool will help you break things down into manageable bites and make a plan for executing them.

If you want the slow and low method, grab a legal pad and pencil (I prefer a whiteboard). Start by brainstorming about everything that has to be done to start operating. Then, put them in an order that resembles a flow chart where items with pre-requisites flow from their parent items. Start with the closest alligator to the boat and when you hit a point on your flow chart that requires you to wait, move to the next top level item and begin that. You'll be moving along before you know it.

An important thing to remember is that you are technically in business now and running a business costs money. Remember the old adage that time is money? That holds true here too. It's not just that wasted time may cost you money and resources; it's also that the longer you are not selling, the longer you are not making money. Time costs in lost opportunity as much as it does in lost revenue. That's not to say that you should rush to jump into selling, but it is to say there is a logical point in your process that certain items will not have to be completed before you can sell. An example would be that you need your website up and running if you are going to sell online. You don't need to have a years worth of shipping materials on hand though. You also don't need a whiz-bang product scanner and UPC software suite in order to sell; you can do that when the volume warrants it.

Piece by piece, it all gets eaten and that's how you get from wanting to do something to actually doing something.

EARS OPEN, MOUTH SHUT

- I don't eat catfish.
- Nothing is too big to accomplish when taken in little pieces.
- Know what the actual requirements are for your business.
- Don't volunteer to be regulated if you don't have to.
- Do it right the first time, even if it takes longer.

Chapter 6

Lesson V

Nice office! How are you going to get out of it?

As entrepreneurs, we all have illusions of grander. The sad fact is that most businesses will fail. It's just the way life is. Sometimes it's because our ideas suck, sometimes it's because the market sucks, sometimes it's because we suck. The bottom line is that something sucks when businesses fail. The question is, how do you prevent that suck from ruining your business, assuming it's not the idea or you, and maybe even ruining your life?

The first thing you have to do is control expenses and that's what this chapter is about. Notice that word again? Control.

Your expenses can kill your business even if you have a great idea and are in a great market. It's simple, really. If you start your business and are selling 10 products a month at $100/each, you have $1000 of revenue. If your spanky new office, copier, computers, phone system, and all the utility bills that go along with that are $5000 a month, you're in trouble.

You probably made a business plan. Remember what you had as revenue forecasts? Good, now forget them. I have never read a new entrepreneurs business plan that wasn't hyper-inflated. When I say hyper-inflated, I'm talking about really, really, off base. With very few exceptions, you are not going to sell out of your initial inventory of 500 widgets in 30 days. I'm sorry to be the one to tell you that, but it happens to be reality. So, with that harsh new reality in hand, rethink what your plan was for facilities and equipment.

If you do need an office space for meetings or compliance with state regulations, can you get away with a shared office space or a short-term rental of a one-room office in a bigger building? If you can, do that. High visibility office and retail spaces are great, when the revenue supports it. They will fill your pantry with noodles and dry spice packs when the revenue isn't there. As a new business, most landlords will require you and your spouse to sign a personal guarantee on top of the business lease, so there's potential that a bad decision here can sink your business and personal finances simultaneously. When I see startups leasing huge, unnecessary spaces, I always think, "How are you going to get out of that lease?" That's because, typically, facility leases are the most expensive part of a small businesses monthly nut and when cash flow is bad, it's also what hurts the most. Beyond that, being stuck in a long, pricey lease will force you to make bad decisions about running your business when money is tight. Instead of spending where you need it, on things like R&D and business development, all of your cash will go to the landlord. Remember, looking big is more important to you than it is to your customers, which includes your office.

Whether you go with a small office or decide to ignore me and go with the huge office on the main road with tons of signs and frontage, you still need to control your other costs. How many phone lines do you need? One. You need one phone line. You don't need ten with an auto-attendant, IP Softphones, after hours call centers, or anything else. I will suggest you actually get a phone number other than your cell phone. You will want to be able to turn that off once in a while and as you grow you'll want to be able to have a phone in the office, should you need an office. There are some free and low cost options out there for doing that, like Google Voice, 8x8, and Skype. With smartphone apps, you can essentially have a second line on your cell phone, but still maintain the ability to not have your cell phone ring all day, every day, with solicitors. The same is true for your home phone. If you work out of your house while you are building your business or simply decide to work from home, you want a phone that's different from your home phone. You may be thinking that your home phone is on the Do Not Call List. Sorry, the moment you use that number as your business number, that no longer applies and you will want to rip it off the wall.

I want to highlight the phones, for a moment more. I see very few businesses make the right decision here. No, I didn't make the right decision the first time either. We think our customers will be impressed if they call our business and have to press buttons while navigating a phone tree to get us. Why is that? I have no idea, but think about it for a moment. Your clients are calling you; they want to speak with you. Is it so bad if they call you and get you directly? How about if they get your voicemail without the ten steps of encryption to get there? If you pick up a phone and call a vendor, are you impressed when you get an automated system? Probably not. If you call them and they answer the phone directly, would you be happier. Probably so.

Speaking of solicitors, you are about to be bombarded by them trying to sell you everything from directory listings to billboards and accounting programs to accountability coaches. If you have a fireplace, that's good, you are also about to increase your junk mail by 100 fold. First off, for the most part, the people calling you are just doing their job. They are trying to earn a living, just like you and me, so there's no need to be a complete jerk to them. Occasionally, the person calling is going to be rude and/or obnoxious. They're actually doing you a favor by being that way. You see, you're going to have all sorts of pent up frustration and angst. Instead of venting on your spouse, kids, family, or friends, go ahead and let loose on these folks. Consider them volunteers for a mad moment of venting. Eventually, you'll get to a point where you don't need that anymore, but in the meantime, enjoy.

I say that somewhat in jest, but not entirely. I mean it when I say not to take it out on the people calling you, they don't deserve it. I also mean it when I say that you are going to experience new levels of frustration and that has to be vented somewhere. Whether you do that at the gym, on a run, or with the people who call you who are obnoxious, you need an outlet. Frustration leads to bad decision making, so decide now how you are going to manage that frustration.

I suggest you adopt a no-decision-while-pissed-off policy. What I mean by that is when you get to a point where your blood pressure is skyrocketing, your face is red, and you want to explode, stop what you are doing. It doesn't matter if you are in the middle of a meeting, on a phone call, or sitting at a computer trying to figure something out. Stop doing it and walk away for a minute. If you can go for a run, a walk, hit the weights, or just grab a drink of water, do something else that's not work even if its just for two minutes. You'll calm down and be able to make better decisions. This is a lot tougher than it sounds, especially if you have a bit of a temper. I'll admit, I have a bit of a temper. I have learned, over the years, to keep that little monster in chains, but every so often it tries to rear its ugly little head. I will also admit that every decision I've ever made while in Hulk mode has been a poor one. These days, I walk away, take 2 minutes, and go back with a clear head. Those 2 minutes will save you hours of apologies and undoing your bad decisions.

Back to the solicitors. As I said earlier, entrepreneurs have a desire to solve problems. You will get calls with purported solutions to all of your problems. It can be very tempting, especially when you are having a problem that the caller claims they can solve. For example, if you're having an issue with low sales volume, it might seem like a message from Heaven when people call you with an offer to sell you leads for individuals and businesses looking for your services. Sounds great, right? The problem is that lead services are generally a really bad idea. You want to find people who need your service and help people find you on their own. You don't want a third party to pull people into registering for information from an industry. These leads are of very low quality, cost a lot of money, and rarely pan out. What you end up doing is spending a lot of time on unqualified leads and ultimately wasting a lot of energy and resources. A better idea might be seeking out, validating, and joining referral networks. These are groups of people in business who have clients with a need they can't fill for geographic reasons or because the service is outside their offerings. These leads are higher quality and worth spending time on.

In all the years I have been doing business, I can recall one time out of the thousands that I really needed the service the caller was offering. More than anything else, that was just a matter of timing. My partner and I just decided we wanted to conduct a media campaign that included radio. The next day, a salesperson from a radio station we discussed called with a promotion. We ended up doing business because they called at the right time and had a plan for integrating their station's advertising into our overall campaign. Other than that, no solicitor ever had something I needed. That's not to say I didn't make the same mistake I am telling you not to. Early on, I bit on a few and wasted plenty of time and money.

As a rule of thumb, if you find you need a service or product, seek it out yourself instead of responding to solicitors. By doing a little research, you'll end up with a better result. If you make a decision to explore or procure a service or product and happen to get a call the next day, don't assign that to divine intervention. You may decide to talk it through with the salesperson, but still do your research on alternatives and make an educated decision.

This ties into controlling costs, because all of the solicitations have a price tag on them. Every time you accept a proposal, you are committing your valuable capital to that product or service. Every time you agree to a term contract, you are increasing your overhead. High overhead and low revenue equals a dead business, so make it a focus of yours to keep your overhead as low as possible no matter what your business plan says your revenue will be.

Overhead is an expansive category of spending. When you consider what your overhead is, it's not just the rent, utilities, and services. Every piece of equipment you buy adds potential to increase your overhead by way of maintenance and material. In order to keep your overhead as low as possible, you have to make some intelligent decisions. Lets take that copier for example, because I made this mistake.

My first business out of the Corps was document intensive. Every deal we put together had pages and pages of contracts. Access to a copier was critical. So, with a nicely padded operating account from our startup investor, we bought a big, complex copier for our office. To my credit, I shopped around and purchased a used one from a copier leasing company. I did know enough to avoid the rental contract associated with the equipment, but that's not saying much considering the thousands we spent on the machine. Sure, we used it, but we also realized it was more cost effective to sign up for the maintenance plan offered by the company that included toner refills and repairs. Can you sense my self-deprecating sarcasm?

It would have been much more cost effective to drive down the street once a day and use the copier at a shipping or office store. At the time, it seemed like the right thing to do because we were working on the assumption that our business plan was more accurate than not. Of course, just like almost every other new entrepreneur, it wasn't and we created overhead for ourselves that we didn't need. It might not have been a lot of money each month, but these things add up quickly and begin to hurt when times are slow.

Fast-forward years later and everything in that business is digital; there's no need for a copier except the rare occasion when a client doesn't have access to the internet. For those occasions, a simple all-in-one printer works perfectly. At least we have an asset we can sell, right. Yeah, right. Copiers depreciate faster than computers do, and that's pretty fast. The technology we purchased wasn't just obsolete in our business; it was obsolete in every business. We had a worthless, car-sized copier that weighed a few hundred pounds and had to be disposed of. In the end, we donated it and closed that mistake out in a fireball of wasted money.

The point is you don't need everything you think you do. There may very well come a time when it makes sense to spend money on equipment that makes your life easier and saves you time. Now is not that time though. Early on, those things tend to cost you more than you think they'll save you. Remember that sweat part? Work a little harder, be a little inconvenienced, and save the money on buying things you don't need right now. If you're business takes off and you want to spend on those things, do it then.

I know I said you should work smarter, not harder, but in the case of equipment, smarter costs money that you should not be spending right now. So, work harder.

EARS OPEN, MOUTH SHUT

• High Overhead kills, keep yours as low as possible.
• The little expenses add up to a big overhead.
• Your business plan projections are probably wrong.
• Pissed? Take 2.
• Skip the pricey equipment, for now.

Chapter 7

Lesson VI

I can't hear you; all the voices in my head sound like B.I.R.D.'s

I don't know any entrepreneurs who stop at one idea. As a breed, ideas are always popping in and out of our heads. Sometimes, the ideas relate entirely to a project we are working on or a business in general. Other times, they are completely unrelated to what we are focusing on, but may still be important. Personally, my mind is always moving and ideas pop in and out faster than I can process them. There are also a lot of demands on my attention: My businesses, my kids, my wife, and even my own competing interests.

I have don't have ADHD, but I do have B.I.R.D.- Business Idea Retention Deficit. Don't go looking for that in a psychology book, I just made it up. It doesn't matter what I'm doing- working, eating, playing, shaving, it literally doesn't matter- ideas are always popping into my mind. If I don't capture an idea within a few seconds, a minute tops, there's a really good chance it's gone. It may be gone for good or it may make another appearance some day, but for all intents and purposes- it's gone.

Beyond losing good ideas, it weighs my mind down. I know I forgot something a few ideas ago, but I can't remember what it was. If something comes to me while I'm in bed getting ready to go to sleep, I won't sleep until I get it into my system so I don't have to worry about forgetting it. This applies equally to tasks that I recognize I have to complete at odd moments in time or activities. With everything else I have going on, I don't need to add to the stress and pressure by not having a system to capture ideas and tasks in order for me not to have to worry about them.

You need a system for capturing and maintaining your ideas and tasks. For me, I have a relatively comprehensive system that I developed over the years and works for me. It may not work for you, but you need to find something that does. There are two essential parts to your system: capturing and organizing.

Since items seem to pop up for me no matter where I am or what I'm doing, I have several different methods for capturing them. The most common for me is sending myself an email. If an idea or task hits me, I immediately pull out my IPhone and send my self a message. Most of the time, I just fill in the subject line with whatever it is I want to remember. If there are details, I may add them in the body. It's quick and simple and it gets the item into my system. I can't always send my self an email though. So, I have ways of capturing these things everywhere. I have a notepad next to my bed, a dive board in my shower (it's like a waterproof Etch-a-Sketch that uses a magnetic pen, yes, really), a pocket size digital recorder in my car, and a pile of index cards on my desk.

All of the functions of those items are pretty obvious, but the index cards may not be. I use index cards all the time to jot down a note about a task or idea. I can then put the card in my physical inbox, my project cache, or my tickler file. It's in my system and I can take action on it when needed. Most importantly, it's out of my head and in my system.

I just mentioned two more aspects of my system that are very important: The Project Cache and the Tickler File. My Project Cache is simply a file folder in my desk drawer that has all of the ideas on projects I want to explore engaging in at some point in time. It is filled with index cards, printed out emails, tear outs from catalogs, and any number of other pieces of material that have ideas I am interested in. I don't want to lose ideas for projects so I capture them and file them in my project cache. Occasionally, I go through that file and discard ideas that I no longer have an interest in or that have been replaced by a more refined idea of the same nature. When I get to a point in my workflow where I have some time to take on a new project, I break out the project cache and choose something to engage. I don't have to worry about forgetting about the idea and I don't spend any time working through the details in my mind until I'm ready to engage it.

The tickler file is something I was first exposed to in the Corps. The admin folks in my first fleet unit used this system and at the time it seemed like there was a better option out there in the form of a digital system. Years later, I read David Allen's "Getting Things Done" and he explained it in detail. I got it, I still get it, and I still use it everyday. It's a very simple system that is very powerful. I was wrong that there was a better digital solution because that would complicate it and make it a pain in the ass instead of a load-lightening tool.

The concept is as basic as it gets. Set aside a drawer in a filing cabinet with hanging folders. If you have to, you can use a desktop hanging folder frame, but part of the beauty is that when you are not using it, it's hidden and out of the way. Get yourself 31 folders of the same color and another 12 of another color. I use 31 red and 12 blue. Buy a label maker and tabs that work with the folders you have, you will need at least 43 tabs.

Create labels for the 31 folders with the numbers 1 through 31; these are your days of the month. Do the same for the 12 folders, using one for each month. Put them in order in your drawer and you now have a tickler file. There are items that need attention on specific days or that you want to address or think about on a specific day. You may have a task you need to complete on a specific day or a bill that needs to get paid on a certain day. You may have a meeting and want to read through some material the day before. Whatever it is that you want to do, read, pay, or think about on a specific day, it goes in that day's folder in your tickler file.

When you sit down at your desk each morning, dump out that day's folder and place the folder in the next month. The front most folder should be a blue folder, which represents the current month. The following folders should be red, representing tomorrow through the end of the month. After that is next months blue folder, followed by all the red day folders that have already passed in the current month. After that are the rest of the blue month folders. When you reach the last day of the current month, you roll the day to the next month as you would usually and also roll the month folder to the back of the month folders.

When something comes up that you want to take care of on a day that is several months ahead, put a sticky note on it with the day you want to address it and put it in that respective months blue folder. When you get to that month, go through that folder and distribute the items to the appropriate red day folders.

Some of you are saying that you have a digital system for tasks that maybe even links to your calendar, phone, IPad, and other devices. That's good, so long as it works. This is the organization part of the system. You are capturing items in a way that works for you and you have a filing system for day specific items and also for your miscellaneous project ideas. Now, you need a way to organize all of the rest of your tasks that you capture. There are many cheap and effective systems for your computer already out there, choose one that works best for you.

For me, I only want to see appointments on my calendar and managing my tasks on there is just painful. I do, however, use a digital system for managing my tasks that don't have to be accomplished on a specific day. These are all of the tasks that I capture throughout my day, but don't have a due date associated. When I plan my Weeks, days, and hours, I pull up my task list and assign them to my time for that week or day. When I have a moment of dead time, which is rare, I also pull up that list and see what I can knock off of it.

In order to be able to effectively do that, all of my tasks are categorized by contexts. Some may require me to be at my desk, some require a phone, others I can do anywhere. This is another concept David Allen teaches and it works very well. The concept is that you will accomplish more and be more efficient if you are able to quickly filter tasks that you can accomplish in your current environment with the tools you have available to you. For example, if you are waiting for the oil to get changed in your car, you can pull out your list and see what you can do in that environment. Perhaps you can make some phone calls, respond to emails, or research something online from your phone. By separating tasks by contexts, you don't waste time sorting through tasks you can't accomplish at that given time and place. It saves frustration and allows you to work efficiently.

When I started my first business, I quickly learned that my old system was broken. Really, I didn't have a system; I had a handwritten calendar. Recognizing I was broken, I searched for better methods. A friend introduced me to the Franklin Covey system and it worked really well for me, for a little while. I ended up taking aspects of that system and adapting it to work for me in the way I worked best. That hybrid worked for a bit too, but it wasn't the ultimate answer. I bounced around trying out different systems. Occasionally, I would integrate an aspect of a new system into mine to make it better. Finally, I was introduced to David Allen's books and by taking some of his concepts, I was able to integrate what already worked with what worked better and the end result was a system that works very well for me.

You need a system, but off the shelf systems may not work for you. I suggest you research several and read some books. Pick those apart and put together a system that works for you. Make sure "Getting Things Done" is on that list of books. You'll also find many options for digital task organization that fit his system by Googling "GTD Program."

EARS OPEN, MOUTH SHUT

• Capture your ideas and tasks.
• You need a context based system for managing tasks.
• Make a tickler file.
• Make a project cache.
• Read "Getting Things Done."
• B.I.R.D. is in your head, even more than Hitchcock's.

Chapter 8

Lesson VII

"Stupid is what stupid does."

Very early on in my days as an Officer Candidate, my Platoon Sergeant made his opinion clear to us about asking questions. He reiterated the often-quoted saying that there "aren't any stupid questions." Common enough, but what he said in follow on is where the genius is, "not asking questions leads to you doing stupid things," or as Forest Gump said, "Stupid is what stupid does."

I'll be the first to tell you that I don't know everything. For you philosophy majors out there, Plato would say that makes me a pretty smart guy. For the rest of us, what that means is that in order to do things that are unfamiliar to me I have three choices: pay someone else to do it for me, learn how to do it myself, or not do it.

There are some things worth paying someone else to do. Whether it's because it's so far outside your wheelhouse, would take too long to learn, or it's simply a pain in the ass, it can pay to pay. Early on in my business, there are very few things I paid other people to do for me. The money just wasn't there for that. As I was growing up and working my way through school, I had many jobs. At the time, it wasn't always a lot of fun missing out on all of the usual debauchery associated with the late teen and college years, but it has paid dividends in my adult entrepreneurial life and suffice it to say I made up for those lost years as a young Lieutenant. I gained experience in a lot of different fields during those years, from graphic design to construction and somewhere in between I even cleaned horse stalls and donned SCUBA gear to repair pools. The point being that I was able to do a lot of the things I needed to get done without outside help.

Further, my exposure to so many different things gave me a solid foundation to build more complex skills on.

In keeping with maintaining a low overhead, if your time and skills permit you to, do it yourself. If your skills allow, but you are slammed with paying customers, then look at the opportunity cost associated with you paying someone to do it versus you doing it yourself and not spending that time with the people who are writing you checks. You'll find there are things you can still do and preserve that precious wad of startup funds.

There are things that you may not need to pay someone to do now, but will in the future. A great example is having an accountant. If you have a small and simple business, say selling something you hand make, you can most likely use a simple books program like QuickBooks Basic and file your taxes using TurboTax. If your business is more complex, it might pay to get yourself an accountant earlier than later. It will cost you, but the more complex your business situation the more likely you'll see savings in your tax liability that surpass what you are paying the accountant and you have someone in your corner who is a subject matter expert (assuming you choose a good accountant). Every little cost adds up to a big expense, so look at each item individually and make an educated decision on what the best move is for you.

There may be a time in the future when you are able to put your entrepreneurial duties through the "Fun Test." That's when you are rolling in the money and want to create more time for things you enjoy doing, be they in your business or outside of it. When that time comes, you can look at all of the things you do within your business and ask yourself whether or not you enjoy doing them. If you enjoy cleaning the toilet in your office with a toothbrush, by all means continue to do that- it's your business. If you don't, hire a cleaning crew or an employee and free that time up for you. If you enjoy hand delivering your product to your customers everyday, keep doing it. If you don't, hire a delivery service. You get the point; there may be a time in your future where you can pay people to do things you don't enjoy. That time isn't now though, sweat a little and save a lot.

If you don't know how to do it, the alternative is learning how to do it. There are a few different ways to accomplish that. You can take a class, read a book, look online, or ask someone who already knows. I'm not a big fan of the taking a class option. I've been there, done that, got the MBA t-shirt. You may have a need for a formal class structure, I find I learn better in a less structured environment where I set the rules and work at my own pace. I am, however, a big fan of books and asking people who already know.

For broader, common topics like learning an accounting system, I would grab a book, or several. For specific items, like finding out how to import products from overseas, ask. An expert in that field can get you smart on what you need to know in a very short period of time and also connect you with people they trust and use for their own business operations. All of my friends and associates know that if I am getting into a business they know something about, I am going to be all over them with questions. They also know I will gladly do the same for them and that they'll get a couple of free meals out of the deal. The information and knowledge you will gain from a 30-minute conversation with someone who knows what they are doing would take you weeks to figure out, not to mention wasted time and energy on bad vendors.

The objections I hear to this are that people don't want to overburden others with their questions or come off as asking stupid questions. To address the first, you'll find most people are more than happy to help you. After all, they get to talk about what they do and, in turn, themselves. Most people like to talk about themselves. Also, you'll find that when you speak to someone who is willing to share their knowledge with you, they are probably surrounded by and work with others that are similar to them. So, when they refer you to someone they work with that you may need to work with as well, you gain another avenue for asking questions. Save your specific questions on that topic for your new connection if you don't want to ask too much. As for the second objection, "Stupid is what stupid does." If you are afraid to ask questions because you feel others may think your questions are stupid, then you're in for some unwarranted sweating- get over that and start asking questions.

I admire people who are self-reliant and try to do things for themselves; it's a quality that serves them well most of the time. Asking questions of others does not sacrifice your self-reliance, diminish your pride, or make you less of a person. If each of us were born with omniscience, life would be no fun and no one would make any money. Each of us has to learn new knowledge and skills to prosper in this world and there are no exceptions. The person you are asking questions of had to learn everything they are telling you at some point too. Certainly, they did not do that in isolation. People helped them along the way by providing their experience, knowledge, and connections. It doesn't mean that when you get help that "you didn't build" your business. It just means you built it the smarter way, not the harder way.

EARS OPEN, MOUTH SHUT

- The questions you don't ask are the only stupid ones.
- Not asking questions makes you do stupid things.
- Don't be afraid to find an expert and ask.
- Sometimes it pays to pay, sometimes you need to do it yourself.

Chapter 9

Lesson VIII

My toe is caught in the stapler.

No matter what anyone tells you, how much you read, or ask questions, there are still things you are going to mess up. That's just part of the process. If you're in to motorcycles, you've probably heard that there are only two types of riders: those who have fallen and those who haven't fallen yet, but will. The same is true for entrepreneurs, if you haven't already messed something up, you will.

What separates former entrepreneurs from current entrepreneurs is how they deal with those mistakes. If you learn from them and make sure you don't make the same mistake twice, you'll be all the better for it. If you keep making the same mistakes over and over again, you fit Einstein's definition of insanity and if it's a big enough mistake it will sink you.

The mistakes we make as entrepreneurs look different in a lot of ways. You may forget to lock a back door, have the wind blow it open, and get a call from the police that requires you to drive 45 minutes in the middle of the night to go lock up and make sure nothing was stolen. Yes, I did that- once, only once. You may make a bad call on a vendor, a product, or advertising campaign. At some point, you will probably hire the wrong person. You are going to do things that are bad for your business based on what you think is the best move at the time, with the information you have available. We all do it.

You are also going to do things that aren't based in sound judgment or even physical coordination. You probably already do these things now, but when you are running your own business, the consequences will seem amplified. These are the little things that happen to us because we're not thinking or paying attention, or just happen because they happen. Think about all of the times you did something and said to yourself, "that was stupid." In most cases, you go about your day and chalk it up as an accident. When you are stressed to the hilt and feel the weight of the world on you, those little things can set the tone for the rest of your day.

Simply accepting the fact that you are going to make mistakes is the first step to coming to terms and, therefor, being able to effectively deal with the consequences. If you approach your business with a complete zero defect policy, every time you make a mistake you will have a tendency to focus on that mistake and miss your greatest opportunities to recover from it. In simple terms, you'll have a one-person pity party that ends up with cigarette burns and a case of empty beer bottles on the floor. That's no good for anyone.

As an entrepreneur, you have to learn to deal with mistakes in a positive way. Every time one is made, an opportunity to learn is created. It doesn't matter how big or small, cheap or expensive, every time a mistake is made you can learn from it. I'm sure you have heard that before- learn from your mistakes. What people have failed to tell you, however, is how to learn from your mistakes. It seems intuitive, but it isn't always. The simple, intuitive, side is, "I made a mistake, and I won't do that again." Easy enough and that certainly does apply to a lot of things. If you stick your hand in a fire and get burned, assuming your nervous system was functioning when you did it, you probably won't do that again; lesson learned. If you stock up on perishable inventory items in anticipation of a demand that never materializes, it might not be so simple.

Using that as an example, at face value, the mistake seems like stocking up on those inventory items. Is that really the mistake you made though? Just as I preach digging to the core issue of a business problem, you also have to dig down to the core cause of the mistake. The fact is that the mistake did not occur in a vacuum. It was the result of an action you took. That action was based on how you operate and that's where your issues are.

You could just not stock up inventory for anticipated demand ever again. That would prevent you from having shelves full of rotting products. But, you very well may find that, because you were "hurt" before, you fail to meet the demand of future customers. If you dig down to why you made the mistake instead of looking at what you did that was a mistake, you will be doing yourself a service and improving your business.

In keeping with our perishable inventory example, and keeping it simple, lets dig down. You took in 5 times the amount of normal inventory as you approached the holiday selling season. You did that because last year you sold 4 times your normal inventory and have seen a 25% increase over last years annual sales. I'm giving you credit for knowing your numbers and analyzing them, which most people don't by the way (another issue entirely). Through your diligent analysis, you have arrived at a stock level that you believe will satisfy demand and clear your shelves. That sounds like pretty sound planning and decision-making.

As the holidays approach, and pass, you find demand never increased to the level you forecasted. When it was all said and done, you only sold 2 times your normal inventory and are therefore left with 60% of your stock sitting on the shelves. There are a lot of reasons why that could have happened. Overall demand could have been depressed, a new product could have entered the market that was better than yours, perhaps there was an issue with your ecommerce platform that you were not aware of. Your mistake wasn't necessarily stocking up on inventory, it was a failure to recognize that you didn't have to. If it was an issue with your ecommerce platform, then your mistake was not monitoring and analyzing the sales and performance data from your site.

The lesson to learn in this case is that you should have based your decision to stock up on inventory, or not, on a combination of information, not just your past performance. Going forward, you can use that experience to better forecast demand and avoid overstocking again as well as under stocking from being too conservative. If you make a sound decision based on the information you have, and that information is well chosen and analyzed, then the decision you make, whether it works well or not, is one that you can support as the best one you could have made; that would not be a mistake.

My last sentence deserves a little more consideration. It's important to understand that not every wrong decision or action will be a mistake; they may just be wrong. What is a mistake and what's just a wrong decision? A mistake is an action, or failure of action, that results in a negative consequence and was arrived at through a faulty decision making process. That means that when you do things you didn't properly think through or failed to think properly about and bad stuff happens, it was a mistake. That "bad stuff" may not be apparent to others, but if you create an internal struggle and have to spend time and energy on working your way out of it, it's also mistake.

A wrong decision is one that is made, to the best of your ability, using correct information, based in a sound process and simply doesn't pan out the way you anticipated. For example, you see a product coming to market that promises to be the best thing since bottled water. The critics are raving, pre-orders are stacking up, and consumers are chomping at the bit. Based on thorough market research and consumer polls, all indications are that the demand will be extraordinarily high for the next six months. The manufacturer is backlogged for 3 months, but you can place an order for stock now and get it in 3 months, which the data shows will still be within the window of extraordinary demand. So, you do it.

3 months later, you get your supply and launch the fact that you have it ready to go for consumers. No one shows up. You sell a few, but nothing close to what you thought you would. It quickly becomes apparent that demand has dried up. Did you make a mistake? No, not at all. You used reliable data sources, did your homework, and made a sound decision. Where you wrong? Yes, you were, but that's okay. We never get it right 100% of the time. Now you would spend some time researching why demand dried up so you can use that in your decision making process next time. Each time you make a mistake or are wrong, so long as you spend the time to dig down into it and find the root cause, you have an opportunity to make yourself and your business better.

From time to time, you are going to get your foot caught in the stapler. How does that happen, you might ask? Great question. I'm not entirely sure, but the lesson I learned personally was to buy a stapler that was too small to fit toes.

EARS OPEN, MOUTH SHUT

- You are going to make mistakes.
- Mistakes are valuable learning opportunities.
- Dig down to the root cause.
- Being wrong doesn't always mean you made a mistake.
- Don't put anything except paper in a stapler.

Chapter 10

Lesson IX

Need more time? Move to Venus.

I am a busy guy by anyone's measure. I have a family to take care of and spend time with, businesses to run, clients to serve, meetings to make, calls to take, walls to paint, and on occasion, personal activities to pursue. I can't remember a day in the past 7 years when I put my head down at night (late at night by the way) and thought to myself, "wow, I got everything done today." We've all heard the saying, "I wish there were more time in the day."

Well, there's good news and bad news. The bad news is that there isn't going to be any more time in a day, unless you move to another planet. I recommend Venus for this purpose, as the days are 243 Earth days long. Yes, it takes 243 Earth days for Venus to complete just one rotation on its axis. One could get a lot done in one Venus day, if they could actually work one day there without experiencing an acute case of death.

The absolute bottom line in life is that nothing we have is more valuable than time. No amounts of money or belongings are more precious than the minutes we have. You can't buy more time, you can't "make" more time, all you can do is use your time as best you can. It is only through time that we are able to do, be, and get the things we want, including family, love, material wealth, experience, etc. I'm not going to tell you what to do with your time; you decide that based on your own personal priorities, goals, and what makes you happy. I am, however, going to propose some things that may help you work better as an entrepreneur, within the time you have.

One of the most challenging things about being an entrepreneur is time discipline. For a majority of us, no one is scowling at us or docking our pay if we show up late for work. No one is standing over our shoulders making sure we punch the clock. It's completely up to us to manage our time effectively so we can accomplish what we need to and still support our priorities. In addition to being one of the most challenging aspects of being an entrepreneur, it's also one of the most rewarding.

Time discipline can be difficult for people who are entering the self-employed world for the first time because they are not accustomed to having near total dominion over their time. It's also hard for seasoned entrepreneurs who take on several businesses or time intensive clients. For both, it's all a matter of how much time to spend doing what.

In a perfect entrepreneurial world, we would all be afforded the luxury of sitting down and being able to complete a given task or series of tasks from beginning to end without interruption. Well, that never happens. The reality is that we have many hats to wear in a single day and not all of them fit well.

Refer back to Chapter 7 where I spoke about capturing and organizing. The first step in managing your time effectively is to have a system. You need to have a plan to tackle each day and come out on top. You may not always finish the race each day, but you'll be able to keep running the next. The tickler file I told you about is part of the system that works for me. Each day I can see tasks and items that need my attention on that particular day. When I am planning out my week, I can refer to my tickler file and see what my date specific task load looks like for that day as well.

You also need a calendar, which probably sounds simple, and it is. It could be a paper calendar or an electronic one. For me, it's electronic and all my devices stay in sync through Apple's flux capacitor. My electronic calendar works for me because I am more mobile than not and I go to meetings with my iPad or laptop, work in the car when someone else is driving, tend to items while I'm waiting for things, and also work from my home office with my desktop. No matter where I am or what I'm doing, I have access to my calendar.

Scheduling appointments and meetings is very similar to retaining tasks in that once you do it they are out of your brain and into your system. Once they are in your system, they no longer weigh your mind down. By always having your calendar with you, you can immediately schedule things and free up some mental RAM. Another benefit of being able to work in this fashion is that it is much more professional to your partners, customers, and associates. No one likes getting off a call or leaving a meeting knowing there needs to be a follow up, but not knowing when or where that will be. It leaves things unsettled and people don't like being unsettled.

With your calendar ready to go, each day you will need to conduct some time planning. Again, how you do that will be different depending on your habits and needs. For me, it's planning every night for the next day and every Sunday for the following week. I plan monthly, quarterly, and annually, typically with stakeholders in my life such as my business partners and family. My weekly planning is often with my wife, so we can fit in the places we can mutually support one another and our kids. The people in your life whom you share priorities and responsibilities with should be included in your planning sessions because you, too, can mutually support one another and work together to reach your goals.

So, what are you planning for? You are creating a framework in which you can work for the coming time period. The shorter the time period, the more granular the plan needs to be. A month may have just the major events you have upcoming, a week should be detailed enough for you execute a schedule, and a daily schedule should be the most granular where nearly every moment of your day is accounted for. For me, each night, I look at my schedule for the following day and fill in between appointments with tasks and functions until my whole day is blocked out. I choose the tasks to populate my day with based on what my priorities are and what projects I want to move forward that day.

As an illustration of the detail I use, here is what a typical day might look like:

0530	Wake up
0530-0600	Breakfast
0600-0645	Run
0645-0715	Run recovery (That means take a shower, etc.)
0715-0730	Kids packed and in car
0730-0800	Take kids to school
0800-0830	Travel time
0830-1000	Gym
1000-1030	Travel time, conference call with John Doe, Inc.
1030-1200	Home Office, forecast for client X (Task)
1200-1230	Lunch at home
1230-1400	Home office, forecast for client X (Task)
1400-1500	Home office, conference call with Jane Smith, LLC
1500-1600	Home office, meeting with Indiana Jones

1600-1700	Home office, return emails and phone calls (Task)
1700-1900	Home, Dinner, Kids time
1900-2000	Kids Bath, Books, Beds
2000-2100	Home office, conference call with West Coast, Inc.
2100-2130	Plan Tomorrow
2130-2230	Read

If I was looking at this day a few weeks ago, I might only see some meetings and conference calls. I will definitely see 1700-1900 blocked out everyday (that's 5pm to 7 pm, by the way). That's my family time. I may go back to work after the kids are in bed or even have to get on a call with the west coast while my wife takes care of that. I may, and often do, work until the wee hours of the morning, but we eat dinner together and play around a bit every night- at least 95% of the time, anyway. The important thing to note is that if I have a commitment that will preclude me from being home between 1700-1900 on any given night, I have to delete my family time to make it fit. I'm not fitting in my family time around my business schedule; I'm fitting my business schedule around my family time. Missing that time at home is the exception.

When I planned my week, I would plug in my runs, gym times, taking the kids, etc. These are the things I would like to get done as part of my personal priorities, but they don't necessarily have to happen on specific days. I like to hit the gym at least 3 times a week, but it doesn't particularly matter what days or at what point in the day. I like to take or pick up my kids to or from school a few times a week, but it doesn't really matter what days and if I can't, I may fit in a lunchtime visit instead.

When I plan the day, I fill in everything else so my whole day is spoken for. It doesn't have to be all work. If I want to read a book, I can plug that in too. Though, for me, that always happens after my schedule is done for the day, i.e. bedtime. I may not meet that schedule exactly on target, but I have a framework to operate within. If I am running early or late, I can make a decision about what to adjust to get back on schedule. I can also make adjustments due to unforeseen circumstances or emerging opportunities. It's your schedule, after all, so you're in control.

EARS OPEN, MOUTH SHUT

• 24 hours in an Earth day, that's just the way it is.
• Capture time requirements and get them into your system.
• Plan with the stakeholders in your life.
• Plan every moment of your workday.
• Schedule hard appointments for personal priorities- work around them.

Chapter 11

Lesson X

U R LOST

There is a standing joke in the Marine Corps about Lieutenants and maps. It goes something like, "the most dangerous thing in the Corps is a Second Lieutenant with a map." The basis of it is that Second Lieutenants aren't very good at land navigation. It really has a much deeper meaning though, that is that young, new officers don't have a whole lot of experience.

The whole idea is probably a little out dated, in all honesty. Certainly, not all Lt's are going to be good at navigating, but all do go through The Basic School (TBS) in Quantico, VA and learn how to navigate. It's something the Corps takes seriously and so do the Lt's, probably because if they fail one of the checks, they have to redo it on a day they would otherwise have had liberty. Young Lt's share many personality characteristics, one of which is the desire to enjoy their youth in the DC Metro area and spend some of their shiny new paychecks on liquid courage. Another, for the most part, is humor.

The land navigation exercises basically consist of being given a starting point and being sent off into the woods to locate several small boxes, often one or more kilometers away. Lt's are given the location of the boxes in a military grid format and have to record the number on the box to prove they found it. It get's even more fun at night, when land features are barely visible and hazards on your chosen path are not visible at all. During more advanced segments, the location of your next "box" is only given as a reference from the one you just found, so if you are wrong, all of your subsequent locations will be wrong as well.

At some point, a group of Lt's thought it would be funny to add some boxes in the woods, but instead of putting incorrect numbers on them, which would hurt their fellow Lt's, they imprinted "U R LOST" on them. If you were to walk by one on your way to your destination, it was quite funny. If you were indeed lost, it was not funny at all.

As young Lt's gain experience and skill in navigation, they really do become quite adept at it, save the few that will just never get it, but that is true no matter the subject or task and is present in any organization. They are learning to identify their current location, a destination, and plot a course between the two. There's more to that than just drawing a line on a map and trying to follow it. In between the two points is wilderness. In order to make it to their destination, they must use the information they have (the map) and plot a course that traverses or avoids natural obstacles. Some of those obstacles may not be as apparently insurmountable as they really are. An example would be a river or stream. The map tells us there is a water source there, it does not account for recent weather or season, however. In the summer, the water may be a foot deep and easily passable. In the spring, after a heavy winter, it may be raging and crossing would be a fatal mistake.

Although Lt's don't realize it when they are trudging through the woods looking for a little metal box with overgrown shrubs hiding it, land navigation training can teach us some valuable business lessons.

You've heard, "if you don't know where you're going, how are you going to know when you get there?" I believe that's true and I preach that, along with other planning paradigms, in Maneuver Management. There is an additional consideration to add to that, however. It doesn't change the fact that you have to have a direction set and destination in mind when you step off on your business operations. It does require you to be able to adapt to changes in the environment and your internal business operations though.

Even when you create your business plan using the best information and research available, things are going to change. Chances are very good that where you end up in 6 months, a year, or 5 years, will look nothing like what you thought it would when you created your initial plan. Being able to adapt is key to your success. Knowing where you are going, or want to go, isn't a one time planning exercise. You must continually plot your position, evaluate it, and make adjustments to either reach your destination or decide on a different destination.

Let's say, for example, you launch a business selling green bracelets. Your plan has you dominating the green bracelet market in 1 year. You have suppliers, distributors, and sales channels all in place and you're off to the races. Six months into it, sales drop off significantly. You discover that consumers no longer want green bracelets; they want red ones. If you stay in the green bracelet business, you probably will be the dominant market player, but you won't have enough sales to keep the business alive. You can reach your goal, but it doesn't make sense to anymore. Because you already have the mechanics in place, you can shift to red bracelet making and compete in that space. You could also try to anticipate what color bracelets the consumers will want next and try to get ahead of the market. In either case, you would be changing your destination, your goal, to fit with reality.

If you're really forward looking and tolerant to risk, you could stop competing on single colored bracelets and create a new product that would open up a new demand. Maybe it's rainbow colored bracelets or maybe it's bracelets made from recycled bracelets. I don't know, but the point is that your destination is going to change and you can adapt or fail. You can also let the market dictate your destination or you can attempt to create your own destination with a new product.

I'm about to clarify something that may sound contradictory to what I teach. I assure you it's not and I'll explain why in a moment. Many people, including me, teach that you should know your end state. That is, again, you have to know where you are going in order to get there. Here's the thing though, that's bullshit.

Okay, bullshit might be a little strong, but the fact is that your end state is going to change many times before you get there and when you do get there you'll realize that your end state is just a milestone. We've all become accustomed to saying, "know your end state," but you can't really know it. You can envision it, create it in your mind, assign feelings to it, and make a plan to make it real. You can't really know it though because you've never been there and its going to change anyway. There are those who say the difference between really successful people and moderately successful or unsuccessful people is that the really successful people have the ability to actually "know" their end state. I'll leave it up to you to decide what you think about that. I'll tell you that I think that's bullshit too. Unless you can time travel, you can't see what your end state actually looks like or feels like; you can't know it.

That said, doing all those things is very important. You do, indeed, have to have a destination to step off on a journey. Without that, you're just wandering. It's not the actual end state that's most important though; it's the process of arriving at that goal and the fact that you have direction in your movement. The ability to adapt as the end state changes is the real key. Don't get me wrong, you need to have your end state, you do. You need that before you begin, but we know it's going to change, so if its not exactly right, so what. Just make sure it's in the same parking lot as the store you are trying to get to.

Don't mistake your end state with your exit strategy. Your end state is what the business looks like in X months, years, or decades. Your exit strategy is what you plan to do when you get there. Maybe you want to sell your business, maybe you want to go public, maybe you shut it down to do something else. Whatever it is, it's what you do with your end state company.

Sometimes, your exit strategy will engage before you reach your desired end state. Lets say, for example, you are building a clothing company and your end state is international distribution with 3 of the major stores. Your exit strategy is to build the company and sell to a larger brand while retaining a royalty on gross sales. After you land your first major store contract, you get an offer from a large brand that fits your end state, so you sell. You accomplished your exit strategy before reaching your end state. Nothing wrong with that.

EARS OPEN, MOUTH SHUT

• Marines have a warped sense of humor.
• Where you are going will change, but you need a starting destination.
• An exit strategy is not an end state, or vice versa.

Chapter 12

Lesson XI

Take the bricks out of your pack; it's heavy enough already.

Part of military training is packing up all your gear and throwing it on your back, then carrying it for long distances. It sucks. Early on in training environments, the trainers dictate all of the gear you pack. A majority of the gear will not serve any purpose during that training evolution, but does serve to add weight and make the hike more challenging. It does that very well.

As you progress through training and enter the regular forces, some of what you are required to carry is dictated, but you also have options for things that will or will not be useful on the mission upon which you are embarking. The things that are dictated to you are often simple items, even some you may believe you can do without. You are told to carry those things because the person telling you has been there before and has the experience to know that it is probably something you will need, regardless of what you may think.

In a training environment, these hikes are especially unpleasant. There are a lot of reasons for that, but one of them is most certainly the amount of gear you are carrying. When you get to choose what gear you bring, it's liberating. It's liberating not only in the sense that you can make some decisions for yourself, but also liberating in a real sense that you gain some physical freedom from unnecessary weight and gear. On the flip side, if you choose not to carry an item, like a jacket, and it gets cold, you can only blame yourself.

In a startup, your business is your pack. You have to lop it up on your shoulders and carry the weight. It will be heavy until you get some traction, and revenue, or you have resources to spread the weight across more people. Ultimately, the weight will still reside on your shoulders, but having some folks to hold up the pack helps relieve the searing pain in your back and allows you to think more freely.

As soon as you pull the trigger on launching your business, you're no longer in training mode. Yes, you will continue to seek knowledge, learn, and grow, but it's on the job training from there on out. You probably have some notions and ideas that you picked up along the way about what you need to do to make your business a success. That's good and some of them will actually help you. A lot of them will not.

There are a lot of resources that tell you what you should fill your business pack with. Heck, I wrote some of them. Not all of the ideas and packing recommendations you get will be right for you. You have to dump your pack out and go through it piece by piece to determine what you really need in there and what can stay behind.

Some of the things you currently have in your pack may serve you well in the future, but right now they are just bogging you down. Think about that Phase III expansion plan you already have built and ready to go. You think about it, read through it, and look at all the pretty pictures you made in PowerPoint to go along with it. Take it out and put it in a footlocker. It will be there when you need it, but right now it's just extra weight.

After you are all set up and your business is running, what is the largest chunk of dead weight in your business pack? It's not you're employees, though they can be a challenge. It's not your systems and processes, though they can slow you down or make you inefficient. It's your customers.

What? My customers? Yes, your customers. I'm sure you have heard the 80/20 rule. It applies here as well. 80 percent of your time will be consumed by 20 percent of your customers. That would be great if they were your best customers, but they won't be. In fact, they'll be the worst customers you have. I know, you're arguing with me in your mind. Go ahead, I understand.

Now that you've worked through the denial phase, start to accept that fact. If you still disagree, just take note and refer back to this a year from now. I see business after business and this is always true. It may not be exactly

80/20, in reality it never is. It is, however, true in principle. A very small number of your customers will consume a majority of your time and they will not be your prime customers.

For the purpose of illustration, let's use the example of a service business such as insurance, mortgage, real estate, or anything of that nature. I'm also going to assume, for this example, that you are capturing and growing a list of clients and customers to build your referrals. Every month, you send out your letter or information packet with relevant and timely information. Then, you follow up with a phone call to your list to make sure they got it and to ask if they or anyone they know has a need for your services.

Some of your folks call you before you get to them and have business for you. Some have a friends name at the ready when you call. Others want to discuss the content of your mailing in great detail and take up an hour of your time each month, but have never sent you any business. If you're asking them for a referral every time you talk and a year goes by without any business, what's the return on investment for your efforts? Not good, that's what it is.

A big mistake new businesses make is holding onto every contact they have and continuing to work that contact month after month for business. They spend money on advertising to them and time trying to pull business out of them. They are dead weight- bricks in your pack. With the time and money you save from not marketing to those individuals anymore, you can go out and develop new contacts and new business. You can also spend more time and money on the people who are your best referral sources.

I suggest rating your clients using a metric that makes sense for you. For this example it might be number of referrals or dollar value of referrals. For a product-based business it might be number of products purchased or dollar value. Maybe, for you, it's a combination of both. Rate them on a scale of 1 to 4 with 1's being the best clients you have and 4's being people who don't generate any money for you.

Increase the value you provide to your 1's to ensure they know you appreciate their business and want to keep them with your business. Instead of a phone call, stop by if you can and ask what you can do for them in their business or life as well. Keep working your 2's and try to make them 1's. Ask your 3's what you can do to serve them better, but don't waste too much time on them. Your 3's are your baseline for marketing. You continue to send them the monthly information, but if after a few follow up calls you're not getting them into the 2's bracket, put them on auto-pilot. Continue the info, but stop the calls.

Every few months you need to evaluate your client list again. Re-assign people into the proper brackets. If someone stays a 3 for two consecutive periods, they become a 4. If a 1 pulls back, they become a 2.

Now, you deal with the 4's. What to do with the people who take your marketing dollars and time and don't provide any business? I bet you already know. You dump the dead weight. Don't be an asshole, just stop marketing to them. If you're really stuck on still letting them know you're alive, keep them on your holiday card list if it makes you feel better, but stop spending money and time every month in a frivolous pursuit of their business. There are a lot of reasons why people end up in your 4 bracket. They may just not like you and not want to send you any business. They may have someone closer to them, like a friend or family member who provides the same thing you do. They may just not have a demand for the product or service you offer. It doesn't really matter what it is that got them into that bracket, what matters is that you free up your dollars and minutes to better serve the people who are sending you business and get out there to develop more.

New and old entrepreneurs alike seem to have an issue with doing this. I guess I can understand why, but it just doesn't make good sense. I've found that when someone gives them permission to drop their dead weight, they do it. Perhaps it's a need for approval, a kind voice saying it's okay. Well, you're not going to find that here. Just do it. You don't need anyone's permission or approval to make your business better. Drop them and move on, you're in control.

Once you're a little lighter and start spending more time on those who are making you money, you'll see increased revenue and a lot less stress. You'll also see that you have a clearer mind to deal with other issues and challenges in your business. Think about an actual pack for a minute, even a regular backpack. If you stuff it full of junk, large and small, when you want something in particular it can seem like it was swallowed by the abyss and you never find it. You can't see it, you can't feel it in there, and you're pretty sure something bit your finger when you were digging around for it.

As you clean that pack out, you'll be able to see more of what's in there and be able to identify the contents. You'll see what bit you was a broken bottle of hot sauce that you forgot you shoved in there before you threw your pack off a cliff. The dead weight does more than eat up your time; it obscures the operations of your business.

There are other forms of dead weight. I mentioned employees, systems, and processes. I said these were not the heaviest dead weight, but they can indeed be heavy. The same concept applies to those things as well. You have to be able to evaluate things in order to make a relative decision. If all of your employees are horrible, then it's probably not your employees that are the problem (it's you, by the way). If you have a process that isn't working, what processes do you have that are working well and why? What can you take from those processes and apply to the other? The rating system metric will change, but not the concept. If you rate a process as a 4, you need to fix it or dump it altogether. If you rate an employee as a 4, they have to go.

There's one giant chunk of waterlogged cardboard that might be weighing down your pack that can be especially difficult to deal with. That's your partner, if you have one. There are too many variables that may apply to your situation for me to cover and make a reasonable and responsible recommendation to you. That is an entire other book. I will tell you that you need to deal with it before it's too late. You need to address the problems and work towards a solution, no matter what that looks like. Unless all of the partners are working towards the ultimate success of the business, on the same path to reach that success, it's not going to work.

I know that, unfortunately, from first hand experience. I can tell you it is very tough to break apart a partnership early in your entrepreneurial life. I can also tell you that you will likely have other more and less formal partnerships down the road and not all of them will work out either. Sometimes you have to grab yourself by the waistband of your Fruit of the Looms and just go your separate ways.

Partnerships are like love, kind of. They are relationships, so that makes sense. What I mean though is in the way they gel or fall apart. You've heard, "You'll know" when referring to when someone will fall in love. Conversely, you've heard people say they knew their love relationship was over a long time ago, but they just dragged it on.

In a partnership, you have the benefit of not having children and an emotional devastation (hopefully), but there's property, money, ownership, etc.- all of which are pretty similar. I digress; the point is that when you are in a relationship, you can tell when things are dead, but still walking. If you're in a partnership that is dead and walking, grab the baseball bat and take it out at the knees before you lose everything. For those of you who might have a hard time seeing my real message, I am not saying that you should go out and hit your partner with a baseball bat, no matter how much you might want to. I am saying that you should get out of an evidently bad partnership before it gets worse.

EARS OPEN, MOUTH SHUT

- Your Business is your pack, keep it light.
- Dump the dead weight.
- Spend time and money where it counts most.
- Clean out the junk.
- A bad partner is worse than no partner at all.

Chapter 13

Lesson XII

"I got nowhere else to go." - Mayo

I hope, for your sake, you launch your business and find immediate success. I know, though, that won't be the case for most of you. You'll have to fight your way through some tough times and every time you have to swing and kick, you'll get more and more tired of swinging and kicking. At some point, you'll think about calling it quits.

Here's where my antithesis of a pep talk comes in: Go ahead, give up; it might be the best business decision you make.

It's true. Giving up might be the best thing you do. I'm not talking about quitting because you've hit a road bump or because you're tired. I'm talking about quitting because if you don't you're going to end up living in a refrigerator box and eating pigeons. You see, part of being a great entrepreneur is knowing when to cut bait and find a new fishing hole. If your business is sucking wind and you're down to your last few months of living expenses, without any indication that you're going to be able to turn things around, it's time to get the hell out of Dodge.

There's no shame in doing that, the shame is in driving it into the ground in a fireball that takes you and your family with it. You live to fight another day and can make another go of it. Even if you have to find a job for a bit to make ends meet until you can regroup and refund, it's the right move.

The key in all of this, of course, is knowing where those decision points are. They are going to be different for everyone depending on risk tolerance, financial situation, ability to gain employment (if needed), family situation, and business type just to name a few. You have to go into your business knowing what those points are for you. Most startup entrepreneurs go into their business with peaches and roses dancing in their heads when they should have developed a plan to continue their life if they fail. Failure happens, so not being ready for it is a bigger failure than any business going under. You can learn a lot from failing in a business, but you don't need to learn the lesson of letting it go too far before getting out. That failure can ruin you.

Stock traders have a tool called a "Stop Loss." Essentially, this is a sell order on a position that is triggered when the stock drops below a pre-designated value. Good traders know their Stop Loss number before they even make a purchase. They also enter their Stop Loss order immediately after they buy the position. In this way, they have committed to selling the position at a loss if their decision to buy was a bad one. They will lose money, but they won't lose everything (in normal trading conditions). If the position they purchased does well, they often move their Stop Loss up with the rising stock price. This is referred to as a "Trailing Stop Loss." The idea being that if the stock makes a turn for the worse, they will not lose all of their profits. Setting a Stop Loss for your business is not only a good idea, it's absolutely critical.

If you are human and your business is struggling, at some point you will have thoughts of quitting. It's normal. Lets assume you haven't reached a Stop Loss point, but are just thinking that you should give this whole thing up. It's important to distinguish between thinking about quitting and wanting to quit.

As I've said, everyone thinks about giving up when times are tough. A line is drawn in the sand for those who think about it and those who want to do it. If you want to give up, you already have and probably should. The decisions you make going forward will not be in the best interest of the business and may not even be logical. Wind down your business and move on. You may not have hit a financial Stop Loss, but you did hit an emotional and psychological one. That doesn't have to mean your entrepreneurial life is over, it's just that business that is over.

Early on in my consulting, I took on businesses that were in desperate situations. I realized pretty quickly that they were already beat; they already quit. In my youthful zeal, I thought I could turn that around. I couldn't, you can't, no one can. I stuffed my pack full of that dead weight I talked about in the last chapter and not even a nuclear powered defibrillator was going to bring them back to life. If someone has already quit on their business and/or themselves, it's all over. The best thing for them, or you, is to get out in a way that preserves as much of the capital they have left as possible.

During that experience, I also found that it was pretty easy to determine whether someone was just thinking of quitting or wanted to quit. I began asking them to think about what their life looked like after they quit, if they did in fact do that. The people who had a well-developed picture were generally already gone. They were probably spending more time thinking about that than they were about their business. The people who had to think about it and search for ideas about what their life would look like were generally still in the game. The exception to that were those people who had been completely defeated. They had no prospects for success in their business, had driven it into the ground, were bankrupt financially and emotionally, and had just given up on absolutely everything. Remember, "U R LOST?" Those folks were very, very lost. They couldn't create a picture of success in their business nor could they create a picture of success after they left their business. That's a bad spot to be in and why I said having a Stop Loss is absolutely critical.

Taken a step further with the people I felt were still with me in the fight, I asked what their business looks like if they stay in it and succeed. Again, a well-developed picture gave me an indication they were even further away from quitting. Lack of that put them closer to the line in the sand.

If you are not sure where you stand, ask yourself the same questions:

- "What does your life look like if you quit?"
- "Do you already have a well developed picture of what that looks like?"
- "Are you happier in that picture?"
- "What about if you didn't quit?"
- "What does your business look like if you make it a success?"

Some good news is coming, but first commit to accepting that you will think about quitting and that it's completely natural in the course of starting and running a business. I've never met a successful person who avoided those feelings and thoughts. The good news is just that- I've never met a successful person who didn't think about quitting at some point. What that means for you is that you're not destined for failure because you're constitution is weak. It's not and you're not. It means that succeeding isn't easy and no one knows that more than the people who have succeeded.

If you recall, early on I said there was a wealth of knowledge out there for you to use to find success. Here's yet another example of that. Not only are there successful people who went through the same personal, emotional, and financial challenges you are going to experience, but they made it through and are willing to tell you how they did that.

You need to seek out the specific knowledge for your industry, but I'll give you a head start that will help you seek out and use that information. How many movies have you seen with a sports team getting their butts kicked and the coach comes in and gives a really inspirational speech that riles the team to victory? Quite a few, I'm sure. What do all of those speeches have in common? They minimize, if not eliminate, doubt.

Of course, these are movies and not real life, but things like that happen every day. They happen in locker rooms and dugouts and they also happen in one-room offices or inside our heads. They may entail a full-fledged speech or be as simple as a shift in the way we are thinking. They eliminate doubt by funneling the energy of wanting to quit into realizing that success is right in front of us and we are the only ones who can reach out and grab it for ourselves. These moments also create acceptance for whatever the result is. Generally, it's the sentiment that if you give it your all and fail, you can hold your head high, but if you give up without trying your hardest, you'll regret it.

I agree with that and believe that you should not be ashamed of failures if you do give it your all or acknowledge success is not on your current path and choose another. You should not regret failing, so long as you learn the lessons contained in failing and acknowledge the failure before the fireball. Whether you want to or not, you will regret crashing and burning when you should have bailed out. You will also regret making the same mistakes the next time.

EARS OPEN, MOUTH SHUT

- Giving up might be the best thing you can do.
- Set your Stop Loss and stick to it.
- Everyone thinks about giving up, lots actually do it.
- If you see failure coming and go out in a fireball, you're an asshole.

Chapter 14

Lesson XIII

May I borrow your pen?

As a small business, you have an advantage that you absolutely need to realize and exploit. You may not have the resources of a big business, but you do have agility. You have the ability to quickly change direction and react to the market. Of course, the goal is to be pro-active, but sometimes reaction is necessary. Most big businesses have huge machines to steer and are slower to change direction. It's like you are a speedboat and big business is a cruise ship. You can turn quickly and maneuver where big business takes half a mile or more to make a significant change in course.

Keep that in mind as you grow. Even when you become a big business, do everything you can to operate with the mentality and agility of a small business. If you do that from step one, you can retain that culture. If you lose it, it will be very painful for you to reinstitute that culture in your big business.

Your agility doesn't just apply to operating within your market; it also applies to your daily functioning. Particularly as a small business, even a one-person shop, you need to be able to do business anywhere. If you read sales books, you'll find each one tells you that you should always have two things on you: business cards and a pen. We find ourselves in an interesting time with technology. Business is largely done electronically, but there are still a lot of people and businesses that rely on paper and pens entirely.

Because of that, you still need to have those two things on you at all times. It doesn't matter if you're at the gym or in a meeting, traveling or having lunch at a deli- you need to always have your business cards and a pen (period). You need to go beyond that now though. You need to have access to your contacts, forms, contracts, email, and files at all times. You need to be able to walk out the door and know you have access to everything you need to close a deal no matter where you are.

Not too long ago, accomplishing that was expensive, complicated, and unreliable. Now, it's cheap, simple, and nearly flawless. You can even carry the ability to share information, be that brochures, sales packets, presentations, or anything else, with you at all times. Getting to the point where you can do all of those things should be critical requirement for you right now, if you haven't already done it.

We accomplish this in our businesses using very simple and inexpensive tools. You already have a computer. I hope it's a Mac, but if it isn't you'll get by until you realize it should be. You should have a smartphone and you should have a tablet. You might say that you already have a laptop, so you don't need a tablet. If your laptop is light, small, and touch screen, you're right. If it isn't, then you need a tablet. I highly recommend having all of your devices on the same operating system; of course that operating system is Mac OS. I say that because you need to be able to sync all of your devices automatically and cross platform syncing is not perfect. Yes, Mac products are more expensive, but they last longer and work better. Spend the extra few bucks and you'll save money and frustration in the long run.

With your mobile devices, you'll be able to quickly respond to emails and calls and keep your business moving as quickly as your customers are. By using a cloud based storage service, like Dropbox, you'll have access to all of your files from your phone, tablet, laptop, and desktop no matter where you are, so long as you have service or Wi-Fi (which is readily available most everywhere). You'll be able to sit in a meeting with clients and immediately share the information they need to make decisions or refer your services to others. You'll be able to pull up contracts and, by using any of the many available applications that let you use your touch screen device to sign documents, close deals on the spot and forward executed agreements immediately to the client and other stakeholders.

Not only does being mobile allow you to move quickly, it also saves you time and energy. By keeping your documents, contracts, and orders electronic, you won't have to waste precious time, or money, making copies and putting together information packages. You won't have to go to the post office or express carrier and mail documents. You'll be more organized, efficient, and professional. Certainly, there will be times when you have to provide hard copies and waste time standing in line to ship things, but that will be the exception and not the rule.

There's nothing worse than meeting a new prospect, no matter where that may be, and not being able to give them your contact information or capture theirs. Nothing worse, that is, other than not being able to close a deal because you need to go back to the office and print out a contract. There's not much better than meeting a new prospect and being able to instantly provide them with all of the information they need to understand your sales proposition. Not much except stopping by to see a client and finding out they need another order and signing it on the spot on your tablet.

To take this another step further, I recommend buying enough storage space in your cloud service to put all of your files on there. That means you are not storing files on your desktop or laptop, but rather all in the cloud. With most services, a copy is retained on your computer, so you have access if you lose internet, so make sure that's the case with the service you are looking at. The reason for this is not just so you have access across all of your devices, but it's also so that when your devices die, you don't get screwed.

If all of your files are in the cloud, and I do mean all of them, when your devices die, you can simply plug in a new device, connect it to your cloud service, and your back up and running. You'll never have that "oh, shit" moment when you realize your device is dead and you've lost your files. Notice, I am saying "when" your device fails and not "if." Your computer equipment will die. It may not be today, but it will die. Yes, even Macs die at some point. They just live much longer, happier, and healthier lives. When it does, you can either be left holding an empty bag and shed a lot of tears, or just get a little pissed that you have to spend money on a new device and go through the hassle of reloading your apps. I choose the latter all day long.

Mobile technology is moving so fast it's incredible. It seems like every day new advances are being made and new tools released. Stay on top of these advances and when refined tools come online that will help you better serve your clients and partners, consider using them. That's not to say jump on board with every new whiz-bang app or program, but when things come online that work well and are integrated with your mobile platforms, test them out and if they work for you, employ them. The "refined" part is crucial. By refined, I mean stable in that it won't crash every time you use it or at a critical moment. I mean integrated, in that it works with your other systems and doesn't only work on one particular OS.

Even though you are on a Mac (hint, hint), not everyone you work with will be. Refined also means that it's easy to use right out of the box, you won't want to train your clients and customers on how to use it and they probably won't want to be trained either. If it's not easy and intuitive, it won't be used.

It's nearly impossible for you and I to anticipate where technology will be in the next few years, if even the next month. Don't get mired down with worrying about being on the absolute leading edge, but don't get left behind either. Everything in moderation, including technology and its application.

Whenever I think about the advances of technology, I can't help but think about NASA. The folks in NASA engineer systems and devices that are nothing short of spectacular. As I watched the newest Mars Rover landing, I was astonished by the perfect integration of the many complicated components that went into making that a success. Then, pictures started rolling in from the Rover. This robotic vehicle was basically taking pictures of itself on another planet with its iPhone and sending them back instantly.

A few days later, I saw an article about the Voyager probes and one of them included a picture recently sent from the edge of the solar system. I had an image of the two control rooms being side by side, the Mars Rover folks in a shiny, new, movie-theater-size room and the Voyager folks in a broom closet. Everyone on the Mars side was cheering and forwarding the pictures the rover had sent back to one another. One of the two guys on the Voyager side shouts, "Hey, Bob, Voyager is sending a picture!" Then, the sound of a 14k modem can be heard with its screeches and scratches and a download status bar appears on circa 1980's computer screen that says, "Time Remaining: 48 Days."

The point being, the technology we have today is so far ahead of what they had back then that the people building those systems could barely have dreamed of it, if at all. In between the two is a graveyard of old, outdated, equipment and programs. Some of which never even saw the light of day because it was obsolete before it was even ready for market.

EARS OPEN, MOUTH SHUT

- Be agile, grasshopper.
- Be mobile.
- Everything in the cloud.
- Always have a pen and business cards, always.
- Stay technologically current and use stable, refined systems.

Chapter 15

Lesson XIV

Race cars go "Vroooooooom."

Imagine a dog sitting in the stands of a race car track with a single car doing laps. Every time the car whips by, the dog perks up as it approaches and the sound of the engine gets louder and louder. It stands up, looking surprised, and tracks the car with its eyes and head as it goes by and the sound fades away. It was genuinely surprised by the sound and behavior of the vehicle. Maybe it even lets out a bark or two.

On the next lap, the dog does the same thing, again genuinely surprised. Next lap, same thing. Every single time the car approaches and passes, the dog is in awe that an object is behaving the way it is. If we could assign words to the dog's body language, it might sound something like, "What's that? Whoa, look at that. What do I do? There it goes! Oh, it's gone." Every lap, the words would be the same.

As people, we find the dog's behavior amusing, maybe even a little endearing. We think it's amusing because we know what the car is and what it's doing. We also know it's the same car, doing the same thing, every lap, and that it will be back around in just a few moments.

New entrepreneurs can be a lot like the dog in my little story. Events occur in the market and they say, "What's that? Whoa, look at that. What do I do? There it goes! Oh, it's gone." Those events could be changes in consumer sentiment, sales opportunities, or anything else that enters and effects the business environment. Even seasoned entrepreneurs will still have this happen on occasion, but what separates the successful ones from the not-so-successful is what they do after it happens.

Successful entrepreneurs, when they miss an opportunity, figure out why. They look for what was behind the change or created the opportunity so they can look for that in the future and not miss it again. If the opportunity is something they feel is important for their business, they make changes in their operations to facilitate being able to capture it on the next lap instead of acting like the ever-surprised dog at the race track.

If you are a reasonably conscious person, it shouldn't take you too many laps to figure out what's going on with the car. That's true in business too. It shouldn't take you too many missed opportunities to realize that you need to figure things out before the next one comes whipping by. Don't mistake that statement and get lazy, thinking you'll have a few freebies before you have to worry about missing changes and opportunities. If those changes are big enough to change the game or the opportunities catapult your competitors into the big leagues, you may not get another chance if you're already against the fence with depleted resources and a struggling business.

Pay attention to the market. Listen to your consumers, partners, and even competitors. I didn't say obey, I said listen. Take it into account and if what you're hearing has merit, act on it. Here's the thing about change and opportunity- it does happen fast, but not too fast for you not to be able to see it coming. Almost everything that will impact your market will have some leading indicators, just like the sound of the car coming in from far off. We may not know exactly what it will look like, but we can know that there is change coming. Staying alert for those indicators is the first step to being able to monetize the changes that occur.

If you go about your daily business with blinders on, all of a sudden, Vrooooom- it passed you by. Maybe you'll take the blinders off, but you have no idea what just happened. If you are looking for those indicators, whatever they may be in your market, even if you're not sure what to do with it, you'll be ready to watch things transpire and use all of the information you gather to improve your performance the next time.

You should be asking yourself when I'm going to tell you what those indicators are. I can tell you there are indicators for wide ranging political, economic, and social changes. The stock market, elections, and buying trends can all be indicators. Your market has micro indicators that I can't tell you, because I don't know what market your in. Ask me about real estate and I'll give you a list. Ask me about business in general and we'll have a long conversation. Ask me to research a market and I'll figure it out. The last one is what you need to do. Yes, I'm going to say it again, because it takes time to sync in- you're not the first to do this. Tap into the wealth of knowledge out there on your specific market and on business in general. Connect with other businesses in your area through networking groups, mastermind groups, and the chamber of commerce. Have conversations and discussions with these people to use the collective experience and knowledge of the group to build a picture of what the market is doing and where it is going. This doesn't have to be formal, go grab a beer with some other business owners and talk through it. Look specifically for people who prospered through the "Great Recession," or better yet the Great Depression. Though the latter is becoming harder and harder as time goes on.

There is a component to this that is very important- you have to retain what you figure out. That is, you have to learn. If the dog had the ability, which it very well may, to figure out that the sound was an indication that the car was coming around again, but then purged it from it's short term memory as soon as the car passed and sound faded, it would be surprised again on the next lap. If the dog had the ability to figure that out, then on the next lap was not surprised, but rather looking for a progression of how this object behaved, he could eventually understand that this one object was a car and it was traveling around this track and the changing sound was a result of the car approaching and passing. Once he got to that point, he would no longer have to be surprised by the car and could instead look for deeper meaning in it. He could try to understand why the car is circling the track. He could try to figure out why the car had such funny colors and pictures on it. He could look beyond the car and see the guy with the clock, timing the car, or the crew waiting to add fuel and change tires. He could, in essence, continue to gain a deeper and deeper understanding of his environment and then make decisions about how he should act. In his case, it might be as simple as whether or not he should be afraid or calm, but in your case it's how you act to take advantage of the situation. For this scenario, that may be as simple as enjoying watching the race. In your business, it's deciding how to operate and be prepared for the next lap.

EARS OPEN, MOUTH SHUT

• Figure out what goes "Vroooom" and why; it will happen again.
• Learn what you find out and continue to develop your understanding.
• Find the indicators and keep a watch out for them.
• When you miss it, figure that out too.

Chapter 16

Lesson XV

Now, open your mouth.

I generally don't read closings in books either. I don't really care how much the author is going to "miss" me or tell me how proud they are of me for getting through the book. So, you're pretty much off the hook, save two things.

Everything in life is cyclical and so it is in business too. That includes the flow of money in and out of your business, the economy, and your stress level just to name a few. New businesses are born everyday and businesses of all ages die everyday. It's the way of the world. The actions you take going forward, based on the decisions you make, will dictate whether or not your business lives or dies.

If you don't look to the experiences of others in books, groups, networking, and any other means of communication to you, you increase your propensity to fail. Business knowledge is gained from experience, but you don't have to experience everything for yourself to learn it. You can learn from others and avoid painful or fatal mistakes. That's part of the business cycle too. People gain knowledge and pass it on to others so they can succeed as well.

As you gain knowledge, share it with your partners and networking groups.

Everyone will benefit, including you. A free and open exchange of lessons learned will help you achieve success and continue to grow. If all those that went before us kept their knowledge to themselves, the world we live in would be a vastly different place than it is today. It's not only our responsibility to pass what we learn on, it's a privilege that should be taken seriously.

You shouldn't teach others because there is a benefit to you. You should do it because it's the right thing to do. On the plus side, however, there is a benefit to you. As you teach others, informally even, you will necessarily develop your ideas and understanding even further and be able to expand your own horizons through that process. It's a great thing for everyone, so do it.

I'll leave you with one final thought. My grandfather told me at a very early age, "Don't ever become what you do for a living. Because, when that's gone, there's nothing left." I have passed that advice on to a lot of people over the years and written it in dozens of pieces. I've seen so many people become what they do for a living, get hurt, lose their job, or retire and end up depressed or dead in a few weeks.

Because their whole identity was based on how they made their living, they felt they lost themselves along with their job. The same holds true for entrepreneurs. Whether you lose your business, have to go back to work, or leave your business for any other reason, realize that your business is your business, not a definition of who you are.

MOUTH OPEN; pass it on.

Dismissed.

www.ingramcontent.com/pod-product-compliance
Lightning Source LLC
Chambersburg PA
CBHW060640210326
41520CB00010B/1687